GOD OF CREATION

A STUDY OF GENESIS 1-11

JEN WILKIN

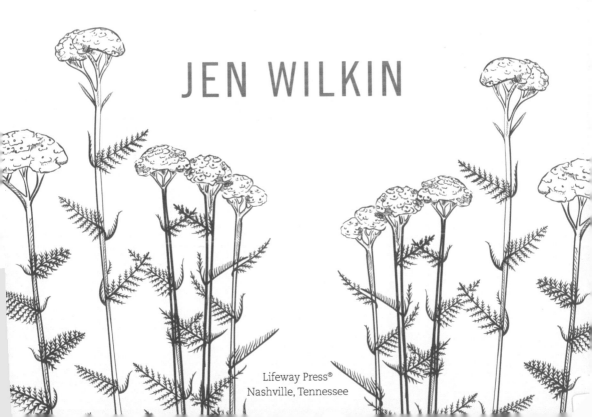

Lifeway Press®
Nashville, Tennessee

Published by Lifeway Press® • © 2017 Jen Wilkin • Reprinted September 2021

ISBN: 978-1-0877-4165-9

Item: 005831464

Dewey Decimal Classification: 231.765
Subject Headings: CREATION \ GOD \ BIBLICAL COSMOLOGY

To order additional copies of this resource, order online at www.lifeway.com; write Lifeway Christian Resources Customer Service: One Lifeway Plaza, Nashville, TN 37234-0113; fax order to 615.251.5933; or call toll-free 1.800.458.2772.

Printed in the United States of America

Adult Ministry Publishing
Lifeway Resources
One Lifeway Plaza
Nashville, TN 37234-0152

CONTENTS

ABOUT THE AUTHOR

Jen Wilkin is a wife, mom to four, and an advocate for women to love God with their minds through the faithful study of His Word. She is a speaker, writer, a teacher of the Bible. Jen lives in Flower Mound, Texas, and her family calls The Village Church home. Jen is the author of *Women of the Word: How to Study the Bible with Both Our Hearts and Our Minds*, *None Like Him: 10 Ways God Is Different From Us (and Why That's a Good Thing)*, *Sermon on the Mount* Bible study, and *1 Peter: A Living Hope in Christ* Bible study. You can also find her at jenwilkin.net.

FOREWORD: HOW SHOULD WE APPROACH GOD'S WORD?

OUR PURPOSE

The Bible study you are about to begin will teach you an important passage of the Bible in a way that will stay with you for years to come. It will challenge you to move beyond loving God with just your heart to loving Him with your mind. It will focus on answering the question, "What does the Bible say about God?" It will aid you in the worthy task of God-discovery.

You see, the Bible is not a book about self-discovery; it is a book about God-discovery. The Bible is God's declared intent to make Himself known to us. In learning about the character of God in Scripture, we will experience self-discovery, but it must not be the object of our study. The object must be God Himself.

This focus changes the way we study. We look first for what a passage can teach us about the character of God, allowing self-discovery to be the by-product of God-discovery. This is a much better approach because there can be no true knowledge of self apart from knowledge of God. So when I read the account of Jonah, I see first that God is just and faithful to His Word—He is faithful to proclaim His message to Nineveh no matter what. I see second that I, by contrast (and much like Jonah), am unjust to my fellow man and unfaithful to God's Word. Thus, knowledge of God leads to true knowledge of self, which leads to repentance and transformation. So are confirmed Paul's words in Romans 12:2 that we are transformed by the renewing of our minds.

Most of us are good at loving God with our hearts. We are good at employing our emotions in our pursuit of God. But the God who commands us to love with the totality of our hearts, souls, and strength also commands us to love Him with all of our minds. Because He only commands what He also enables His children to do, it must be possible for us to love Him well with our minds or He would not command it. I know you will bring your emotions to your study of God's Word, and that is good and right. But it is your mind that I am jealous for. God intends for you to be a good student, renewing your mind and thus transforming your heart.

OUR PROCESS

Being a good student entails following good study habits. When we sit down to read, most of us like to read through a particular passage and then find a way to apply it to our everyday lives. We may read through an entire book of the Bible over a period of time, or we may jump around from place to place. I want to suggest a different approach, one that may not always yield immediate application, comfort, or peace, but one that builds over time a cumulative understanding of the message of Scripture.

READING IN CONTEXT AND REPETITIVELY

Imagine yourself receiving a letter in the mail. The envelope is handwritten, but you don't glance at the return address. Instead you tear open the envelope, flip to the second page, read two paragraphs near the bottom, and set the letter aside. Knowing that if someone bothered to send it to you, you should act on its contents in some way, you spend a few minutes trying to figure out how to respond to what the section you just read had to say. What are the odds you will be successful?

No one would read a letter this way. But this is precisely the way many of us read our Bibles. We skip past reading the "envelope"—Who wrote this? To whom is it written? When was it written? Where was it written?— and then try to determine the purpose of its contents from a portion of the whole. What if we took time to read the envelope? What if, after determining the context for its writing, we started at the beginning and read to the end? Wouldn't that make infinitely more sense?

In our study, we will take this approach to Scripture. We will begin by placing our text in its historical and cultural context. We will "read the envelope." Then we will read through the entire text multiple times, so that we can better determine what it wants to say to us. We will read repetitively so that we might move through three critical stages of understanding: comprehension, interpretation, and application.

STAGE 1: COMPREHENSION

Remember the reading comprehension section on the SAT? Remember those long reading passages followed by questions to test your knowledge of what you had just read? The objective was to force you to read for detail. We are going to apply the same method to our study of God's Word. When we read for comprehension we ask ourselves, "What does it say?" This is hard work. A person who *comprehends* the account of the six days of creation can tell you specifically what happened on each day. This is the first step toward being able to interpret and apply the story of creation to our lives.

STAGE 2: INTERPRETATION

While comprehension asks, "What does it say?," interpretation asks, "What does it mean?" Once we have read a passage enough times to know what it says, we are ready to look into its meaning. A person who *interprets* the creation story can tell you why God created in a particular order or way. She is able to imply things from the text beyond what it says.

STAGE 3: APPLICATION

After doing the work to understand what the text says and what the text means, we are finally ready to ask, "How should it change me?" Here is where we draw on our God-centered perspective to ask three supporting questions:

- What does this passage teach me about God?

- How does this aspect of God's character change my view of self?

- What should I do in response?

A person who *applies* the creation story can tell us that because God creates in an orderly fashion, we too should live well-ordered lives. Knowledge of God gleaned through comprehension of the text and interpretation of its meaning can now be applied to my life in a way that challenges me to be different.

SOME GUIDELINES

It is vital to the learning process that you allow yourself to move through the three stages of understanding on your own, without the aid of commentaries or study notes. The first several times you read a passage, you will probably be confused. This is actually a good thing. Allow yourself to feel lost, to dwell in the "I don't know." It will make the moment of discovery stick.

Nobody likes to feel lost or confused, but it is an important step in the acquisition and retention of understanding. Because of this, I have a few guidelines to lay out for you as you go through this study:

1. **Avoid all commentaries** until *comprehension* and *interpretation* have been earnestly attempted on your own. In other words, wait to read commentaries until after you have done the homework, attended small-group time, and listened to the teaching. And then, consult commentaries you can trust. Ask a pastor or Bible teacher at your church for suggested authors. A list of commentaries used to create this study can be found on page 186.

2. For the purposes of this study, **get a Bible without study notes.** Come on, it's just too easy to look at them. You know I'm right.

3. Though commentaries are initially off-limits, here are some **tools you should use:**

   • **Cross-references.** These are the Scripture references in the margin or at the bottom of the page in your Bible. They point you to other passages that deal with the same topic or theme.

   • **An English dictionary** to look up unfamiliar words.

   • **Other translations of the Bible.** We will use the English Standard Version (ESV) as a starting point, but you can easily consult other versions online. I recommend the New International Version (NIV), New American Standard Version (NASB), or the New King James Version (NKJV). Reading more than one translation can expand your understanding of the meaning of a passage. Note: a paraphrase, such as The Message, can be useful but should be regarded as a commentary rather than a translation. They are best consulted after careful study of an actual translation.

   • **A printed copy of the text,** double-spaced, so you can mark repeated words, phrases, or ideas. This will be provided in your notebook as needed.

STORING UP TREASURE

Approaching God's Word with a God-centered perspective, with context, and with care takes effort and commitment. It is study for the long-term. Some days your study may not move you emotionally or speak to an immediate need. You may not be able to apply a passage at all. But what if ten years from now, in a dark night of the soul, that passage suddenly opens up to you because of the work you have done today? Wouldn't your long-term investment be worth it?

In Matthew 13, we see Jesus begin to teach in parables. He tells seven deceptively simple stories that leave His disciples struggling for understanding—dwelling in the "I don't know," if you will. After the last parable, He turns to them and asks, "Have you understood all these things?" (v. 51). Despite their apparent confusion, they answer out of their earnest desire with, "Yes" (v. 51). Jesus tells them that their newfound understanding makes them "like the owner of a house who brings out of his storeroom new treasures as well as old" (13:52, NIV).

A storeroom, as Jesus indicates, is a place for keeping valuables over a long period of time for use when needed. Faithful study of God's Word is a means for filling our spiritual storerooms with truth, so that in our hour of need we can bring forth both the old and the new as a source of rich provision. I pray that this study would be for you a source of much treasure and that you would labor well to obtain it.

Grace and peace,

Jen Wilkin

HOW TO USE THIS STUDY

This Bible study book is designed to be used in a specific way. The homework in the Bible study book will start you down the process of comprehension, interpretation, and application. However, it was designed to dovetail with small group discussion time and the teaching sessions. You can use the Bible study book by itself, but you are likely to find yourself with some unresolved questions. The teaching sessions are intended to resolve most, if not all, of your unanswered questions from the homework and discussion time. With this in mind, consider using the materials as follows:

- If you are going through the study **on your own**, first work through the homework, and then watch or listen to the corresponding teaching for that week.

- If you are going through the study **in a group**, first do your homework, and then discuss the questions your group decides to cover. Then watch or listen to the teaching. Some groups watch or listen to the teaching before they meet, which can also work if that format fits best for everyone.

Note: For Week One, there is no homework. The study begins with an audio or video introduction. You will find a Viewer Guide on pages 14-15 that you can use as you watch or listen to the introductory material.

HOW TO USE THE LEADER GUIDE

At the end of each week's personal study you will find a Leader Guide intended to help facilitate discussion in small groups. Each guide begins with an introductory question to help group members get to know each other and feel comfortable contributing their voices to the discussion.

These questions may prove to be most helpful during the early weeks of the study, but as the group grows more familiar with one another, group leaders may decide to skip them to allow more time for the questions covering the lesson.

The remainder of the Leader Guide includes four questions to help group members compare what they have learned from their personal study on Days Two through Five. These questions are either pulled directly from the personal study, or they summarize a concept or theme that the personal study covered. Each two-part question covers content from a particular day of the personal study, first asking group members to reflect and then asking them to apply. The reflection questions typically ask group members to report a finding or flesh out an interpretation. The application questions challenge them to move beyond intellectual understanding to identify ways to live differently in light of what they have learned.

As a small group leader, you will want to review these questions before you meet with your group, thinking through your own answers, marking where they occur in the personal study, and noting if there are any additional questions that you might want to reference to help the flow of the discussion. These questions are suggestions only, intended to help you cover as much ground as you can in a 45-minute discussion time. They should not be seen as requirements or limitations, but as guidelines to help you prepare your group for the teaching time by allowing them to process collectively what they have learned during their personal study.

As a facilitator of discussion rather than a teacher, you are allowed and encouraged to be a co-learner with your group members. This means you yourself may not always feel confident of your answer to a given question, and that is perfectly OK. Because we are studying for the long-term, we are allowed to leave some questions partially answered or unresolved, trusting for clarity at a later time. In most cases, the teaching time should address any lingering questions that are not resolved in the personal study or the small-group discussion time.

WEEK ONE:
GENESIS INTRODUCTION

Who wrote the Book of Genesis?

Moses may have written Parts of genesis

When was it written?

6th & 5th century BC
1550 BC

To whom was it written?

Doesn't say but it's inclined
Toward the Israelites

In what style was it written?

"high style" Parallelism
Hebrew Poetry

What is the central theme of the book?

Describing God
Fall of human line

Creation
Sibling rivalry
Infertility
Covenants
lies of deceit.

WEEK TWO:

THE GOD WHO WAS IN THE BEGINNING

The opening lines of Genesis teach us some of the most foundational truths about God. In them, we find the answers to some very big questions. And we raise some pretty big questions too.

Romans 1:20 tells us that "since the creation of the world *God's invisible qualities—his eternal power and divine nature—have been clearly seen*, being understood from what has been made" (NIV, emphasis mine). The creation story of Genesis has truths to teach us about the character of God, and it begins teaching them in the very first sentence:

In the beginning, God created the heavens and the earth.
GENESIS 1:1

WHO CREATED?

In the beginning, **GOD** *created the heavens and the earth.*

The first verse of Genesis makes clear that God is the Creator of heaven and earth. The Bible attributes all creation to God and God alone. This is a significant statement because it speaks definitively against other explanations of creation.

1. Think through what you know of history, other religions, and current scientific thought on the origins of the universe. How might someone with a non-biblical worldview fill in the statements below?

    "In the beginning, _____ created the heavens and the earth."

    "In the beginning, _____ created the heavens and the earth."

2. How is it significant that in Genesis God alone is given credit for the act of creation? Why do you think Moses, the leader of the nation of Israel, would choose to start his narrative by declaring that God alone created? (Hint: Read Exodus 20:1-3.)

3. Look up John 1:1-4. Compare it to Genesis 1:1-2. Sneak a peek at Genesis 1:3-4 as well. What similarities do you see between the two passages? In the space below, note any words, phrases, or ideas that the two passages share.

Look through both passages and note who was present at creation.

_____*God*_____ (Gen. 1:1)

__*God + Spirit*____(Gen. 1:2)

__*Christ, the Word*"__(John 1:1)

READ ROMANS 1:18-25.

4. Note below specifically how Paul says humankind sinned against God (v. 21).

5. Paul lists at least five outcomes of this sin. Note them below:

  1.

  2.

  3.

  4.

  5.

6. **APPLY:** Why do you think failure to acknowledge and worship God as Creator is a sin? What sinful behaviors might result from this sin?

In contrast, how does acknowledging and worshiping God as Creator cause us to live righteous lives? What godly behaviors might result from this belief?

WHAT DID GOD CREATE?

In the beginning, God created
THE HEAVENS AND THE EARTH.

7. What do you think is included in the phrase *the heavens and the earth?*
    Look up Colossians 1:16-17, and note what Paul says God created in the
    chart below.

THINGS GOD CREATED	THINGS GOD DID NOT CREATE

What do you think Paul is saying in verse 17? Rewrite it in your
own words.

8. **APPLY:** How does the knowledge that God created all things—the earth, our solar system, the universe, the atom, the electron, all life, all matter—how does that knowledge change the way you think about God? (Look up Psalm 24:1-2 for a little help. David mentions the earth, but he could just as easily have said "the heavens" or "all creation." Why?)

How should the knowledge that God created all things change the way you regard and treat His creation?

HOW DID GOD CREATE?

*In the beginning, God **CREATED** the heavens and the earth.*

9. How does Genesis 1:1 say that God created the heavens and the earth? Note below all scientific data, timelines, materials, and equipment recorded.

10. Look up the following verses, and note what each says about how God created.

    PSALM 33:6,9

    REVELATION 4:11

While these verses shed some very important additional light on the *how* of creation, they don't offer us the nuts and bolts of what actually took place to bring it about. Christians have developed and hotly debated a number of explanations for the *how* of creation, among them:

THEISTIC EVOLUTION
   ▢ Evolution was the process that God used to bring about the Earth as we know it.[1]

□ The Earth is approximately 4.5 billion years old, as evidenced in the fossil record and astronomical data.[2]

□ The six days of creation refer to epochs of evolutionary development.[3]

YOUNG EARTH CREATIONISM

□ The Earth is between six thousand and ten thousand years old.[4]

□ The fossil strata were laid down in the flood of Noah, which was global in scope.[5]

□ God created the world in six literal days.[6]

OLD EARTH CREATIONISM

□ God created the universe through a combination of natural processes and direct intervention.[7]

□ The Earth is approximately 4.5 billion years old, as evidenced in the fossil record and astronomical data.[8]

□ The six days of creation need not be taken literally as 24-hour periods.[9]

Put a check mark next to any of these explanations that you are familiar with.

Much has been written on the different views of creation. We will not be spending time exploring them, but I strongly encourage you to do so on your own, especially if only one of the views is familiar to you.

11. Obviously, if God had wanted to disclose the process of creation, He could have done so. Why do you think He chose not to? List some possible reasons below.

12. Look up the word *create* in the dictionary. Read through the various definitions and then write one below that best describes how God creates.

CREATE:

What is the key difference between the definition you chose and the ones you did not?

WHEN DID GOD CREATE?

IN THE BEGINNING, *God created the heavens and the earth.*

13. What do you think is meant by the phrase *in the beginning?* What, exactly, is *beginning* in the beginning?

14. Glance back at Romans 1:20. What two examples of God's invisible qualities that we can learn from creation does Paul give?

    Which of those two do we learn by reading that God created *in the beginning?*

15. Look up the word *eternal* in a dictionary or thesaurus. In your own words, write a definition for it that best fits the way it describes God.
    ETERNAL:

16. Now look up the following verses, and note how each supports your definition of the *eternality* of God. (It may be helpful to copy them down.)

PSALM 90:1-2

PSALM 102:12,25-27

ISAIAH 48:12-13

17. If God is eternal and creation exists within time, what or who existed *before* the beginning? Make a complete list below:

18. **APPLY:** How does the understanding that God is eternal change the way you think about your life? How is His eternality a comfort?

WHY DID GOD CREATE?

19. Many theories have been put forth as to why God created the heavens and the earth and especially why He created humans. Below are a few commonly given reasons. Look up the reference next to each statement, and note how it confirms or denies what the statement claims.

    God created the universe because He was lonely.

    JOHN 1:1; 17:5

    God created humans so He could have an object for His love.

    JOHN 3:34-35

    God created humans because He needed helpers to accomplish His will.

    ACTS 17:24-25

    God created because He was bored, unfulfilled, or any other human state of mind.

    PSALM 50:21a

20. Now look up the following verses, and note why they say God created the heavens and the earth.

PSALM 19:1-4

PSALM 148:1-5

21. **APPLY:** It is much easier to rule out reasons why God created than it is to identify them. God created to display His glory. God created because it pleased Him to do so. Beyond that, we are left to marvel at the mystery. Looking back over questions 19 and 20, what false idea of why you exist do you sometimes walk in? How does rejecting that idea lead to healthier belief?

WRAP-UP

Note: Each week we will end our homework by focusing on what the text has revealed about God. A list of God's attributes can be found in the back of your Bible study book (p. 184) to help you think through your answer to the wrap-up questions.

What aspect of God's character has this week's passage of Genesis shown you more clearly?

Fill in the following statement:
Knowing that God is _____ shows me that I am
_____.

What one step can you take this week to better live in light of this truth?

INTRODUCTORY QUESTION: What part of God's creation causes you to marvel the most?

1. **OBSERVE:** (question 2, p. 18) How is it significant that in Genesis God alone is given credit for the act of creation? Why do you think Moses, the leader of the nation of Israel, would choose to start his narrative by declaring that God alone created? (Hint: read Exodus 20:1-3.)

    APPLY: (question 6, p. 19) Why do you think failure to acknowledge and worship God as Creator is a sin? What sinful behaviors might result from this sin?

    In contrast, how does acknowledging and worshiping God as Creator cause us to live righteous lives? What godly behaviors might result from this belief?

2. **OBSERVE:** (question 7, p. 20) What do you think is included in the phrase *the heavens and the earth*? Look up Colossians 1:16-17, and note what Paul says God created. What do you think Paul is saying in verse 17?

    APPLY: (question 8, p. 21) How does the knowledge that God created all things change the way you think about God?

    How should the knowledge that God created all things change the way you regard and treat His creation?

3. **OBSERVE:** (question 15, p. 25) Look up the word *eternal* in a dictionary or thesaurus. In your own words, write a definition for it that best fits the way it describes God.

    APPLY: (question 18, p. 26) How does the understanding that God is eternal change the way you think about your life? How is His eternality a comfort?

4. **OBSERVE:** (question 19, p. 27) Many theories have been put forth as to why God created the heavens and the earth and especially why He created humans. Which of the theories noted in question 19 (p. 27) have you heard or been taught?

APPLY: (question 21, p. 28) It is much easier to rule out reasons why God created than it is to identify them. God created to display His glory. God created because it pleased Him to do so. What false idea of why you exist do you sometimes walk in? How does rejecting that idea lead to healthier belief?

5. **WRAP-UP:** What aspect of God's character has this week's passage of Genesis shown you more clearly?

Fill in the following statement:
Knowing that God is _____ shows me that I am
_____.

What one step can you take this week to better live in light of this truth?

WEEK TWO | VIEWER GUIDE NOTES

WEEK THREE:

SIX DAYS AND A REST

This week the curtain goes up on the great story of Genesis. In its opening scene, we find God doing what He does best: bringing light after darkness, order after chaos, rest after toil, all through the power of His Word.

Begin your week's study by reading through Genesis 1:1–2:3 as though you are seeing it for the first time. Read it in the ESV and the NIV, keeping in mind the author, purpose, style, and historical context of Genesis. Then answer the questions that follow.

DAY ONE
IN THE BEGINNING ...

READ GENESIS 1:1-2.

> [1] *In the beginning, God created the heavens and the earth.* [2] *The earth was without form and void, and darkness was over the face of the deep. And the Spirit of God was hovering over the face of the waters.*

1. In Genesis 1:2, how would you describe the state we find the earth in? Use your own words. Read the verse in the ESV (above) and NIV to help you.

2. Who is mentioned as being present on the earth?

3. Look up the verses below, and note what each tells you about the role of the Spirit. What does the Spirit do?

    JOB 33:4

    PSALM 104:24-30

JOHN 6:63

ROMANS 8:11

4. Keeping in mind what is about to happen in Genesis 1:3-31,
    why do you think the Spirit is hovering over the waters in 1:2?

DAY TWO
THE SIX DAYS OF CREATION

READ GENESIS 1:3-31.

You will need colored pencils and a copy of the text to complete this section of the lesson. The text is included at the end of the homework this week (p. 47).

5. On the chart below, mark a check in the box by each day of creation that you find a particular phrase occurs. Mark each phrase as you find it in the text by underlining it with the same color each time it occurs (i.e. mark *And it was so* with a red underline, *God called* with a blue underline, etc.).

CREATION PHRASE	DAY ONE	DAY TWO	DAY THREE	DAY FOUR	DAY FIVE	DAY SIX
"God said, 'Let (there be) …'"						
"And it was so … "						
"And God saw that it was good."						
"God called … "						
"And there was evening and there was morning, the ___ day."						

6. Why do you think Moses uses repetition to tell the story of the six days of creation? List several possible reasons below or in the margin.

7. Why do you think Moses chose to repeat these particular phrases? Write the idea you think each phrase is meant to convey in the space next to it.

CREATION PHRASE	IDEA IT CONVEYS
"God said, 'Let (there be) … '"	
"And it was so …"	
"And God saw that it was good."	
"God called …"	
"And there was evening and there was morning, the ___ day."	

8. Look back through the text and circle the word *God* (or the personal pronoun *He*) in **green** each time it occurs. What part of the sentence does the word *God* occupy throughout this narrative? (Circle your answer below.)

Subject   *Verb*   *Object*

9. Count how many times God (or the personal pronoun He) occupies the subject of the sentence: _____ Why do you think Moses writes the creation story in this way? What does he want us to be very clear about?

10. **APPLY:** The cosmos obeys the commands of our God, yielding to His will without hesitation or resistance. What clear command of God causes you to hesitate or resist? How does the creation account instruct you to respond?

DAY THREE

11. Now look through the text (p. 47), and circle the word *separate* or *separated* in **orange** each time it occurs. In the boxes below, put a check next to each day that the concept of separation takes place. (Hint: It may be implied.) Also note what is separated.

	DOES SEPARATION OCCUR?	WHAT IS SEPARATED?
Day One		
Day Two		
Day Three		
Day Four		
Day Five		
Day Six		

12. Moses wants us to understand in the earliest passages of Genesis that God is a God who separates. Read Leviticus 20:22-26. (ESV translation is most clear here.) Remember that Moses wrote Leviticus so that the Israelites would carry God's Law in written form into the promised land. Note specifically who or what is separated in this passage.

13. Is separation a concept that was important only for Old Testament believers to understand? Read the following New Testament passages, and note how the concept of separation applies to us today.

2 CORINTHIANS 6:14-18

EPHESIANS 4:31-32

HEBREWS 4:12-13

14. **APPLY:** How would God have you embrace a call to separation from that which does not honor Him? From what sin or situation do you need to separate yourself?

DAY FOUR
THE SEVENTH DAY

READ GENESIS 2:1-3.

15. How does the language of the seventh day compare to that of the other six days? Does it follow the same pattern?

16. What is different about what happens on the seventh day versus what happened on the other six?

17. Rather than pronouncing that the seventh day was "good" or "very good," what does God pronounce on the seventh day (2:3)?

   "God _____ the seventh day and made it
   _____."

The phrase *made it holy* can also be said *set it apart*. The God who separates sets aside the seventh day for a specific purpose.

18. What did God do on the seventh day (2:2)?

   Did God rest because He was tired?   Yes   No

   Look up the following verses and note how each supports your answer.

   PSALM 121:1-4

   ISAIAH 40:28

19. Read Exodus 20:8-11. It contains the fourth of the Ten Commandments. Write below what it asks Israel to do and why.

The word *Sabbath* literally means *rest*, specifically from work. The seventh day of creation is the first day of Sabbath, "because on it God rested [sabbathed] from all his work that he had done in creation" (Gen. 2:3).

20. **APPLY:** Practically, how should we live out obedience to the fourth of the Ten Commandments in our daily living? Give some specific ways below.

As with all of God's commands, Sabbath is for our benefit. What benefits come from observing Sabbath in our lives?

21. Compare Genesis 2:2-3 to John 19:28-31a. Fill in the chart below.

	WHO HAS BEEN WORKING?	WHAT WORK IS FINISHED?	WHAT DAY FOLLOWS THE COMPLETION OF THE WORK?
Genesis 2:2-3			
John 19:28-31a			

22. Read Matthew 11:28-30. Answer the questions below.

Who is speaking? _____

What does He offer those who are weary? (See v. 29—be specific.)

_____

Why do you think they are weary? Why would someone's soul need rest?

What work has Jesus done that allows Him to offer rest, not merely to our bodies, but to our souls?

23. Now read Ephesians 2:8-9. Note what it says about work. Can we find Sabbath for our souls on our own?

24. Also read Psalm 62:5-6 (NIV). What admonition does David give to himself?

25. **APPLY:** How are you tempted to work for the approval of God? What is preventing you from resting in the finished work of Christ? What vain work do you need to rest from?

WRAP-UP

What aspect of God's character has this week's passage of Genesis shown you more clearly?

Fill in the following statement:
Knowing that God is _____ shows me that I am
_____.

What one step can you take this week to better live in light of this truth?

GENESIS 1

[1] In the beginning, God created the heavens and the earth. [2] The earth was without form and void, and darkness was over the face of the deep. And the Spirit of God was hovering over the face of the waters.

[3] And God said, "Let there be light," and there was light. [4] And God saw that the light was good. And God separated the light from the darkness. [5] God called the light Day, and the darkness he called Night. And there was evening and there was morning, the first day.

[6] And God said, "Let there be an expanse in the midst of the waters, and let it separate the waters from the waters." [7] And God made the expanse and separated the waters that were under the expanse from the waters that were above the expanse. And it was so. [8] And God called the expanse Heaven. And there was evening and there was morning, the second day.

[9] And God said, "Let the waters under the heavens be gathered together into one place, and let the dry land appear." And it was so. [10] God called the dry land Earth, and the waters that were gathered together he called Seas. And God saw that it was good.

[11] And God said, "Let the earth sprout vegetation, plants yielding seed, and fruit trees bearing fruit in which is their seed, each according to its kind, on the earth." And it was so. [12] The earth brought forth vegetation, plants yielding seed according to their own kinds, and trees bearing fruit in which is their seed, each according to its kind. And God saw that it was good. [13] And there was evening and there was morning, the third day.

[14] And God said, "Let there be lights in the expanse of the heavens to separate the day from the night. And let them be for signs and for seasons, and for days and years, [15] and let them be lights in the expanse of the heavens to give light upon the earth." And it was so. [16] And God made the two great lights—the greater light to rule the day and the lesser light to rule the night—and the stars. [17] And God set them in the expanse of the heavens

to give light on the earth, [18] to rule over the day and over the night, and to separate the light from the darkness. And God saw that it was good. [19] And there was evening and there was morning, the fourth day.

[20] And God said, "Let the waters swarm with swarms of living creatures, and let birds fly above the earth across the expanse of the heavens." [21] So God created the great sea creatures and every living creature that moves, with which the waters swarm, according to their kinds, and every winged bird according to its kind. And God saw that it was good. [22] And God blessed them, saying, "Be fruitful and multiply and fill the waters in the seas, and let birds multiply on the earth." [23] And there was evening and there was morning, the fifth day.

[24] And God said, "Let the earth bring forth living creatures according to their kinds—livestock and creeping things and beasts of the earth according to their kinds." And it was so. [25] And God made the beasts of the earth according to their kinds and the livestock according to their kinds, and everything that creeps on the ground according to its kind. And God saw that it was good.

[26] Then God said, "Let us make man in our image, after our likeness. And let them have dominion over the fish of the sea and over the birds of the heavens and over the livestock and over all the earth and over every creeping thing that creeps on the earth."

[27] So God created man in his own image,
    in the image of God he created him;
    male and female he created them.

[28] And God blessed them. And God said to them, "Be fruitful and multiply and fill the earth and subdue it, and have dominion over the fish of the sea and over the birds of the heavens and over every living thing that moves on the earth." [29] And God said, "Behold, I have given you every plant yielding seed that is on the face of all the earth, and every tree with seed in its fruit.

You shall have them for food. [30] And to every beast of the earth and to every bird of the heavens and to everything that creeps on the earth, everything that has the breath of life, I have given every green plant for food." And it was so. [31] And God saw everything that he had made, and behold, it was very good. And there was evening and there was morning, the sixth day.

GENESIS 2:1-3

[1] Thus the heavens and the earth were finished, and all the host of them. [2] And on the seventh day God finished his work that he had done, and he rested on the seventh day from all his work that he had done. [3] So God blessed the seventh day and made it holy, because on it God rested from all his work that he had done in creation.

WEEK THREE I GROUP DISCUSSION

INTRODUCTORY QUESTION: What is your favorite part of the day and why?

1. **OBSERVE:** (question 6, p. 38) Why do you think Moses uses repetition to tell the story of the six days of creation?

   APPLY: (question 10, p. 40) The cosmos obeys the commands of our God, yielding to His will without hesitation or resistance. What clear command of God causes you to hesitate or resist? How does the creation account instruct you to respond?

2. **OBSERVE:** (question 13, p. 42) Is separation a concept that was important only for Old Testament believers to understand? Read the following New Testament passages, and note how the concept of separation applies to us today: 2 Corinthians 6:14-18; Ephesians 4:31-32; Hebrews 4:12-13.

   APPLY: (question 14, p. 42) How would God have you embrace a call to separation from that which does not honor Him? From what sin or situation do you need to separate yourself?

3. **OBSERVE:** (question 19, p. 44) Read Exodus 20:8-11. It contains the fourth of the Ten Commandments. What does it ask Israel to do and why?

   APPLY: (question 20, p. 44) Practically, how should we live out obedience to the fourth of the Ten Commandments in our daily living? Give some specific ways.

   As with all of God's commands, Sabbath is for our benefit. What benefits come from observing Sabbath in our lives?

4. **OBSERVE:** (question 23, p. 45) Read Ephesians 2:8-9. Note what it says about work. Can we find Sabbath for our souls on our own?

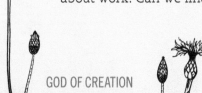

APPLY: (question 25, p. 46) How are you tempted to work for the approval of God? What is preventing you from resting in the finished work of Christ? What vain work do you need to rest from?

5. **WRAP-UP:** What aspect of God's character has this week's passage of Genesis shown you more clearly?

Fill in the following statement:
Knowing that God is _____ shows me that I am
_____.

What one step can you take this week to better live in light of this truth?

WHAT THE CREATION NARRATIVE WANTS TO TELL US:

1	4
2	5
3	6

7

WEEK FOUR:

CREATED IN THE IMAGE OF GOD

This week we will explore the significance of the creation of man and woman. How were they created? What were they created to do? How are they distinct from the rest of creation?

At the end of your homework, the text for this week is printed for you (p. 65). We will start by examining the sixth day of creation as it is described within the six-day creation narrative (Genesis 1:24-31). Then we'll look at the expanded description of the creation of humankind found in Genesis 2:4-25.

DAY ONE

READ THROUGH GENESIS 1:24-31.

1. Mark every occurrence of the word *image* or *likeness* in **green**.

    Glance back through the other five days of creation. What other creatures are created in God's image?

2. If the skies, mountains, plants, and animals were not created in God's image, what do you think it means that humans are created in the image or likeness of God? In what ways are we different (set apart/separate) from the rest of creation? How do humans uniquely reflect the image of their Creator in ways that the rest of the creation does not?

3. Look back at the text and mark every occurrence of the words *have dominion over* or *subdue* in **blue**. Why do you think God gives humans dominion over all the creatures of the earth?

4. Look back at Genesis 1:26-28. Mark each occurrence of the word *them* in **orange**. Why does Moses use the pronoun *them* instead of *him*?

5. To which pronoun (*them* or *him*) is the designation of ruler given? What can you conclude from this?

6. What point is emphasized three times in 1:27? Why do you think Moses did this?

7. Read 1:29-30. Note what type of diet is provided for humans and animals.

   What is included? _____

   What is excluded? _____

   Why do you think this is so?

8. **APPLY:** Bearing in mind that God pronounces the creation "good," how were humans intended to be good rulers over all the creatures of the earth? What are the qualities of a good ruler?

   How do the qualities you listed mirror the way that our good God rules us?

DAY TWO

NOW SHIFT YOUR FOCUS TO GENESIS 2:4-25.

9. Genesis 2:4 begins with "These are the generations of (NIV: *This is the account of*) the heavens and the earth when they were created ..." What is your initial reaction to this introductory sentence?

10. Does the account of the creation of humans appear to be told chronologically (in sequential order)? Give an example to support your answer.

11. In Genesis 2, Moses is going to re-tell the creation story from a different vantage point. If he bothers to tell us something twice, we need to pay close attention to any changes in this second account. Compared to Genesis 1, how would you describe the re-telling of the creation story in Genesis 2? (Circle your answers.)

SCOPE OF GENESIS 2:	Covers all six days	Covers a specific portion	
TEMPO OF GENESIS 2:	Faster	The same pace	Slower
SUBJECT OF GENESIS 2:	God	The land and creatures	Man
STYLE OF GENESIS 2:	More poetic	More scientific	Less poetic
RHYTHM OF GENESIS 2:	More repetitive	Same amount of repetition	Less repetitive

12. Why do you think Moses makes these changes to his writing? Try to put yourself in the position of storyteller, and think about why you might adjust your style at different points in your narrative.

13. What do you notice about the way God is referenced? How does it change in chapter 2?

Chapter 1: _____

Chapter 2: _____   _____

The title for God in Genesis 1 is *Elohim* (your text simply says *God*), a word referring to Him as God Almighty. In chapter 2, we see *Elohim* combined with *Yhwh* (your text says the LORD God). *Yhwh*, or *Yahweh*, as we tend to see it written, is the personal name of God, the *I AM* that God says to Moses in Exodus 3.

14. Does God seem more personal in Genesis 2? Which of His words or actions lead you to your conclusion?

15. **APPLY:** Is it easier for you to conceive of God as almighty or as personal? What past experiences or relationships in your life have influenced how you answer?

DAY THREE

NOW LOOK MORE CLOSELY AT GENESIS 2:4-17.

16. In 2:8-9, we have our first description of the garden that God plants in the region of Eden. Next week we will watch a drama unfold there. For this week, note below what you learn about the different trees in the garden. Next to each, write why you suspect God has placed it in the garden.

TREE(S)	PURPOSE
" ... every tree that is pleasant to the sight and good for food ... "	
the tree of life	
the tree of the knowledge of good and evil	

17. Read 2:10-14. Which of the landmarks that Moses gives for the garden's location are you familiar with?

Which are unfamiliar to you?

Why do you think Moses includes this section of the text? What purpose does it serve? Give your best answer.

18. In 2:15-17 we learn about humans' roles and restrictions within the garden. What are they?

ROLES:

RESTRICTIONS:

19. Why do you think God gives man and woman specific roles?

Why do you think He gives them restrictions?

20. **APPLY:** God is a good ruler who knows what He is doing. Roles and restrictions can be difficult, but they are also good. Think of a role and a restriction God has placed upon you. In the space below, note what makes them hard but ultimately good.

	DIFFICULT BECAUSE	GOOD BECAUSE
ROLE		
RESTRICTION		

DAY FOUR

NOW LOOK MORE CLOSELY AT GENESIS 2:18-25.

21. Though God has heretofore pronounced " ... and it was good ... " over His creative work, what jarring statement does He make in verse 18? What solution does He propose?

22. If the man has God and the animals for companionship, in what way(s) is he alone?

23. What do you think is meant by "fit helper"? In what ways will woman be suitable to help man that the rest of creation cannot? (Hint: She reflects the image of her Creator in ways the rest of creation does not.)

24. In verses 19-23 mark each occurrence of the terms *name* or *called* with an underline.

    In Genesis 1, who is naming various aspects of the creation?

    _____

    In Genesis 2, who takes on this role? _____

    Why do you think God gives the man this task?

25. In what ways do you think a husband and wife become "one flesh"?

26. Think about the implications of being one flesh. Read Ephesians 5:28-31. How do you care for your own flesh? What does this say about how we should treat a spouse?

27. Read Genesis 2:25. Why do you think Adam and Eve are comfortable with their nakedness prior to the fall?

28. **APPLY:** Though Genesis is historical narrative and not a fairy tale, Moses is definitely setting the scene for the drama that will play out in chapter 3. We might say this is his "once upon a time" section of the unfolding history. Based on what you know will happen in chapter 3, in three sentences summarize chapter 2 in your own words. Use the voice of a storyteller speaking to a child.

Once upon a time,

WRAP-UP

What aspect of God's character has this week's passage of Genesis shown you more clearly?

Fill in the following statement:
Knowing that God is _____ shows me that I am
_____.

What one step can you take this week to better live in light of this truth?

GENESIS 1:24-31

[24] And God said, "Let the earth bring forth living creatures according to their kinds—livestock and creeping things and beasts of the earth according to their kinds." And it was so. [25] And God made the beasts of the earth according to their kinds and the livestock according to their kinds, and everything that creeps on the ground according to its kind. And God saw that it was good.

[26] Then God said, "Let us make man in our image, after our likeness. And let them have dominion over the fish of the sea and over the birds of the heavens and over the livestock and over all the earth and over every creeping thing that creeps on the earth."

[27] So God created man in his own image,
in the image of God he created him;
male and female he created them.

[28] And God blessed them. And God said to them, "Be fruitful and multiply and fill the earth and subdue it, and have dominion over the fish of the sea and over the birds of the heavens and over every living thing that moves on the earth." [29] And God said, "Behold, I have given you every plant yielding seed that is on the face of all the earth, and every tree with seed in its fruit. You shall have them for food. [30] And to every beast of the earth and to every bird of the heavens and to everything that creeps on the earth, everything that has the breath of life, I have given every green plant for food." And it was so. [31] And God saw everything that he had made, and behold, it was very good. And there was evening and there was morning, the sixth day.

GENESIS 2:4-25

⁴ These are the generations

  of the heavens and the earth when they were created,

  in the day that the LORD God made the earth and the heavens.

⁵ When no bush of the field was yet in the land and no small plant of the field had yet sprung up—for the LORD God had not caused it to rain on the land, and there was no man to work the ground, ⁶ and a mist was going up from the land and was watering the whole face of the ground— ⁷ then the LORD God formed the man of dust from the ground and breathed into his nostrils the breath of life, and the man became a living creature. ⁸ And the LORD God planted a garden in Eden, in the east, and there he put the man whom he had formed. ⁹ And out of the ground the LORD God made to spring up every tree that is pleasant to the sight and good for food. The tree of life was in the midst of the garden, and the tree of the knowledge of good and evil.

¹⁰ A river flowed out of Eden to water the garden, and there it divided and became four rivers. ¹¹ The name of the first is the Pishon. It is the one that flowed around the whole land of Havilah, where there is gold. ¹² And the gold of that land is good; bdellium and onyx stone are there. ¹³ The name of the second river is the Gihon. It is the one that flowed around the whole land of Cush. ¹⁴ And the name of the third river is the Tigris, which flows east of Assyria. And the fourth river is the Euphrates.

¹⁵ The LORD God took the man and put him in the garden of Eden to work it and keep it. ¹⁶ And the LORD God commanded the man, saying, "You may surely eat of every tree of the garden, ¹⁷ but of the tree of the knowledge of good and evil you shall not eat, for in the day that you eat of it you shall surely die."

[18] Then the LORD God said, "It is not good that the man should be alone; I will make him a helper fit for him." [19] Now out of the ground the LORD God had formed every beast of the field and every bird of the heavens and brought them to the man to see what he would call them. And whatever the man called every living creature, that was its name. [20] The man gave names to all livestock and to the birds of the heavens and to every beast of the field. But for Adam there was not found a helper fit for him. [21] So the LORD God caused a deep sleep to fall upon the man, and while he slept took one of his ribs and closed up its place with flesh. [22] And the rib that the LORD God had taken from the man he made into a woman and brought her to the man. [23] Then the man said,

"This at last is bone of my bones
     and flesh of my flesh;
she shall be called Woman,
     because she was taken out of Man."

[24] Therefore a man shall leave his father and his mother and hold fast to his wife, and they shall become one flesh. [25] And the man and his wife were both naked and were not ashamed.

WEEK FOUR I GROUP DISCUSSION

INTRODUCTORY QUESTION: Of all the tasks you are responsible for, which is your favorite and why?

1. **OBSERVE:** (question 5, p. 57) To which pronoun (*them* or *him*) is the designation of ruler given? What can you conclude from this?

   APPLY: (question 8, p. 57) Bearing in mind that God pronounces the creation "good," how were humans intended to be good rulers over all the creatures of the earth? What are the qualities of a good ruler?

   How do the qualities you listed mirror the way that our good God rules us?

2. **OBSERVE:** (question 14, p. 59) Does God seem more personal in Genesis 2? Which of His words or actions lead you to your conclusion?

   APPLY: (question 15, p. 59) Is it easier for you to conceive of God as almighty or as personal? What past experiences or relationships in your life have influenced how you answer?

3. **OBSERVE:** (question 19, p. 61) Why do you think God gives man and woman specific roles?

   Why do you think He gives them restrictions?

   APPLY: (question 20, p. 61) God is a good ruler who knows what He is doing. Roles and restrictions can be difficult, but they are also good. Think of a role and a restriction God has placed upon you. What makes them hard but ultimately good?

4. OBSERVE: (question 26, p. 63) Think about the implications of being one flesh. Read Ephesians 5:28-31. How do you care for your own flesh? What does this say about how we should treat a spouse?

APPLY: (question 28, p. 63) Based on what you know will happen in Genesis chapter 3, in three sentences summarize chapter 2 in your own words. Use the voice of a storyteller speaking to a child: *"Once upon a time ..."*

5. WRAP-UP: What aspect of God's character has this week's passage of Genesis shown you more clearly?

Fill in the following statement:
Knowing that God is _____ shows me that I am
_____.

What one step can you take this week to better live in light of this truth?

WEEK FOUR | VIEWER GUIDE NOTES

WEEK FIVE:

PARADISE LOST

At the end of Genesis 2, we found ourselves in a perfect garden, an ordered creation pronounced unequivocally good by its Creator. But human experience tells us that we are far from such a place now. In Genesis 3, we are given an explanation for the brokenness, sorrow, and travail that are the common experience of all who have lived on God's green earth. It is a story as familiar as temptation itself, but it is not a story devoid of hope.

DAY ONE

READ GENESIS 3:1-24.

1. Think back to Genesis 1 and 2. For each chapter, write a one to three sentence summary of what happens.

   GENESIS 1

   GENESIS 2

2. How do the first two chapters of Genesis set the stage for the events that take place in Chapter 3?

DAY TWO

NOW LOOK MORE CLOSELY AT 3:1-6.

3. The temptation of Eve teaches us a few things about the way we ourselves can be tempted by the enemy. What do you think the serpent was trying to achieve by asking "Did God actually say ... " in 3:1?

    How might someone today experience a similar temptation?

4. How should we respond to such a question? Look up the following verses to help you with your answer:
    PSALM 19:7-14

    PSALM 119:11

    LUKE 4:3-4

5. Take a closer look at what God actually said and what Eve replies to the serpent's question. Fill in the chart below with what each said.

WHAT GOD SAID	WHAT EVE SAID GOD SAID
Genesis 2:16	Genesis 3:2
Genesis 2:9 (Note what God put in place.)	Genesis 3:3
Genesis 2:17	Genesis 3:3

Which of God's words does Eve downplay?

Which of God's words does Eve amplify?

What do Eve's words reveal about her attitude toward God?

6. Read 3:4-5. What tactic does the serpent employ next to alienate Eve from God?

How might someone today experience a similar temptation?

7. How do you think Eve should have responded to the serpent?

8. What three characteristics of the fruit attracted Eve to it (3:6)?

    1.

    2.

    3.

    Were these things bad to desire? What was wrong with pursuing these things by eating the fruit?

    How might someone today experience a similar temptation?

9. What do you think Adam should have done when Eve offered him the fruit?

10. The serpent told Eve that eating the fruit would make her like God (3:5). In what way was this true (3:22)? In what way was it a lie?

11. **APPLY:** In what area(s) of your life are you wrestling or flirting with temptation right now?

How does the account of Adam and Eve's temptation give instruction to you on resisting yours?

DAY THREE

NOW LOOK AT 3:7-13.

12. Notice how sin affects Adam and Eve's actions. Next to each passage, note what they do and why you think they do it.

	WHAT ADAM AND EVE DO AS A RESPONSE TO THEIR SIN	WHY THEY REACT THIS WAY
Genesis 2:25; 3:7		
Genesis 3:8-10		
Genesis 3:12-13		

13. God asks a series of questions of Adam and Eve (3:9-13). Look up Psalm 139:1-4. In light of how this passage describes God, what do you think is His reason for asking questions instead of using some other form of dialogue?

14. **APPLY:** Which of the ways Adam and Eve respond to their sin have you used yourself? What wrong belief about God causes you to respond that way?

DAY FOUR

NOW LOOK AT 3:14-19.

15. Scan through the passage, and note the occurrence of the word *cursed*. Note below the verses where you find it and upon what/whom a curse is pronounced.

16. In your own words, paraphrase God's response to the actions of the serpent. What will be different from now on (3:14-15)?

    Why do you think God assigns this particular consequence for the serpent? How is it a fitting one?

17. In your own words, paraphrase God's response to the actions of the woman. What will be different from now on (3:16)? Look back at 2:18 to help with your answer.

    Why do you think God assigns this particular consequence for the woman? How is it a fitting one?

18. In your own words, paraphrase God's response to the actions of the man. What will be different from now on (3:17-19)? Look back at 2:15-17 to help with your answer.

Why do you think God assigns this particular consequence for the man? How is it a fitting one?

19. **APPLY:** Based on what transpires between the serpent and our parents, Adam and Eve, how would you define *sin*?

NOW LOOK AT 3:20-24.

20. What is Adam's first recorded act after the consequences of sin have been laid out (3:20)? How does this act signify hope?

21. What is God's first recorded act after the consequences of sin have been laid out (3:21)? How does this act signify hope?

22. God expels Adam and Eve from the garden to prevent further devastation. What does He not want to happen? Why (3:22-23)?

23. What security measure does God put in place to ensure that His garden will not be violated (3:24)? _____
    Look up the following verses to see other places these angelic creatures are mentioned in Scripture. Next to each reference, note the location where they are depicted.

    EXODUS 36:8

    NUMBERS 7:89

PSALM 99:1

EZEKIEL 10:18-19

How would you describe their role?

24. Based on the story of Genesis 3, how has God's relationship with humans been altered as a result of sin?

25. **APPLY:** How does God's response to the sin of Adam and Eve warn you? How does it reassure you?

WRAP-UP

What aspect of God's character has this week's passage of Genesis shown you more clearly?

Fill in the following statement:

Knowing that God is _____ shows me that I am

_____.

What one step can you take this week to better live in light of this truth?

INTRODUCTORY QUESTION: What is your favorite "forbidden treat" to eat?

1. **OBSERVE:** (question 7 & 9, p. 77) How do you think Eve should have responded to the serpent? What do you think Adam should have done when Eve offered him the fruit?

   APPLY: (question 11, p. 78) In what area(s) of your life are you wrestling or flirting with temptation right now?

   How does the account of Adam and Eve's temptation give instruction to you on resisting yours?

2. **OBSERVE:** (question 13, p. 79) God asks a series of questions of Adam and Eve (3:9-13). Look up Psalm 139:1-4. In light of how this passage describes God, what do you think is His reason for asking questions instead of using some other form of dialogue?

   APPLY: (question 14, p. 79) Which of the ways Adam and Eve respond to their sin have you used yourself? What wrong belief about God causes you to respond that way?

3. **OBSERVE:** (question 17 & 18, pp. 80-81) In your own words, paraphrase God's response to the actions of the woman and the man. What will be different from now on?

   Why do you think God assigns the particular consequences He does? How are they fitting?

   APPLY: (question 19, p. 81) Based on what transpires between the serpent and our parents, Adam and Eve, how would you define *sin*?

4. **OBSERVE:** (question 24, p. 83) Based on the story of Genesis 3, how has God's relationship with humans been altered as a result of sin?

   APPLY: (question 25, p. 83) How does God's response to the sin of Adam and Eve warn you? How does it reassure you?

5. **WRAP-UP:** What aspect of God's character has this week's passage of Genesis shown you more clearly?

   Fill in the following statement:
   Knowing that God is _____ shows me that I am
   _____.

   What one step can you take this week to better live in light of this truth?

WEEK FIVE | VIEWER GUIDE NOTES

WEEK SIX:

CAIN AND ABEL

In Genesis 3, we watched our parents live out the fundamental definition of sin: placing our wills above God's will. This week we will look at the fallout of their defiant act. We'll see how quickly sin took hold within only one generation. Clinging to the promise that God would crush the serpent through the seed of the woman, Adam and Eve become the first parents. But parenting outside the garden of God's provision proves to be thorn-laden toil.

DAY ONE

READ GENESIS 4:1-16.

1. In Genesis 3, who is sinned against?
    Humankind against _____

    In Genesis 4, who is sinned against?
    Humankind against _____

    Humankind against _____

2. Summarize the main point of the story of Cain and Abel in one sentence:

3. How does this portion of the narrative connect logically to what happened in the previous chapter?

DAY TWO

TAKE A CLOSER LOOK AT 4:1-3.

4. Read 4:1-2 in the ESV and NIV. What does Eve say at the birth of Cain?

    Why do you think she says this? Look back at 2:21-22 to help you with
    your answer.

5. Now look at 1 Corinthians 11:11-12. How does it add to your
    understanding of what Eve means in 4:1?

6. What were the occupations of Eve's first two sons?

    Cain: _____

    Abel: _____

    How do their occupations fit with what we learned in Genesis 1–3
    about the role of humans in creation?

    Based on Genesis 1–3, is one of these occupations more honorable than
    the other?

7. Though this scene pre-dates the giving of the Law, the brothers make what resembles the firstfruits offerings the Law later required of the people of God (as we will see later in our study). Note below what each brother offered. Be specific.

Cain: _____

Abel: _____

8. **APPLY:** From a spiritual standpoint, how does giving God the first and best of our labors orient our hearts rightly to Him? What would be a practical example of how a modern-day believer could follow the same principle?

DAY THREE

NOW LOOK AT 4:4-7.

9. Cain and Abel both present offerings to God, but for some reason, one brother finds favor, and the other does not. Look up the following verses and note what insight they give into whether each offering follows a pattern of "acceptable worship."

DEUTERONOMY 26:1-11 *(especially vv. 2,10)*

EXODUS 13:2,12

EXODUS 34:19

LEVITICUS 3:14-16

Based on these verses, what seems the most likely reason Cain's offering was rejected by God?

10. Now look up Psalm 51:14-17. What possible help does this passage give us for understanding Cain's rejected sacrifice?

11. Look closely at Genesis 4:5. Is Cain's offering the only thing that does not find favor with God?

12. Look up the following verses, and note how they explain God's rejection of not just the worship but the worshiper.

    1 SAMUEL 16:7

    PSALM 40:6-8

    HEBREWS 11:4,6

Based on these verses, what is the most important element of any act of worship?

13. Look again at 4:5. What is Cain's emotional response to being rejected?

   _____

   What would have been a correct response?

14. **APPLY:** Like Cain, how are we sometimes guilty of offering sacrifices to God that are unacceptable in His sight? Give an example from your own life.

   Why do you think we have a tendency to do this?

NOW LOOK AT 4:6-12.

15. How is God's handling of Cain's sin similar to his handling of Adam and Eve's sin? List all similarities below.

16. Look again at 4:9. How is Cain's verbal response to his sin similar to that of Adam and Eve?

    How is it different?

17. Although God does not answer Cain's question in 4:9, what is the obvious answer? _____

18. Look up 1 John 3:11-15. What emotion does John associate with Cain's murderous actions in verse 15? _____

    Below is the Great Command (Luke 10:27) with the word *love* removed from it. Substitute the word you wrote above into the blanks:

    You shall _____ the Lord your God with all your heart, soul, mind, and strength, and you shall _____ your neighbor as yourself.

    How is this reversal of the Great Command an accurate portrayal of Cain's story?

19. Look at Genesis 4:11-12. What is Cain's punishment for murdering his brother?

How is Cain's punishment a perfect fit, not just for the crime, but for the criminal?

20. **APPLY:** What does it mean to affirm that we are "our brother's keeper"? Who should the modern-day believer view as a brother or sister?

What person in your sphere of influence are you resistant to treat with preferential love, as a brother or a sister? What fear, justification, or sinful attitude holds you back? What steps can you take to master your resistance, by the grace of God?

DAY FIVE

NOW LOOK AT 4:13-16.

21. Based on his response, did Cain repent of his sin (4:13-14)? Explain your answer.

22. Why do you think God marks Cain to prevent him from being killed?

23. What do you learn about God's character from the way He deals with sin in the story of Cain and Abel? List specific character traits below and where you find them in the story.

24. Read Matthew 5:21-24. To what act does Jesus link the emotion of anger in this passage?

    What does Jesus say about acceptable offerings?

25. We have focused on Cain quite a bit, but what about Abel? Look up Hebrews 11:4, and note what it tells us about Abel.

26. According to the author of Hebrews, Abel's blood still speaks to us today because of his faith. Beside each statement about Abel in the chart below, look up the passage, and note what New Testament figure aligns with his story.

ABEL ...		... AND SO WAS ...
... was a shepherd.	John 10:11	
... was hated by a brother for no cause.	John 15:23-25	
... was the object of his brother's jealousy.	Matthew 27:15-18	
... was violently slain by his brother.	Acts 2:22-23,36	
... offered an acceptable sacrifice.	Ephesians 5:2	

Based on your answers above, what brother has answered *yes* to the question of whether He is your keeper?

27. **APPLY:** Because he did not deal with it when God warned him to, Cain's anger toward God and anger toward his brother degraded into violence and murder.

With whom are you most likely to get angry?

What would God have you do with your anger? By grace, how can you respond to it as Cain should have?

WRAP-UP

What aspect of God's character has this week's passage of Genesis shown you more clearly?

Fill in the following statement:
Knowing that God is _____ shows me that I am
_____.

What one step can you take this week to better live in light of this truth?

INTRODUCTORY QUESTION: What is your favorite family tradition?

1. **OBSERVE:** (question 6, p. 93) What were the occupations of Eve's first two sons? How do their occupations fit with what we learned in Genesis 1–3 about the role of humans in creation? Based on Genesis 1–3, is one of these occupations more honorable than the other?

   APPLY: (question 8, p. 94) From a spiritual standpoint, how does giving God the first and best of our labors orient our hearts rightly to Him? What would be a practical example of how a modern-day believer could follow the same principle?

2. **OBSERVE:** (question 12, p. 96) Look up the following verses, and note how they explain God's rejection of not just the worship but the worshiper: 1 Samuel 16:7; Psalm 40:6-8; Hebrews 11:4,6. Based on these verses, what is the most important element of any act of worship?

   APPLY: (question 14, p. 97) Like Cain, how are we sometimes guilty of offering sacrifices to God that are unacceptable in His sight? Give an example from your own life. Why do you think we have a tendency to do this?

3. **OBSERVE:** (question 18, p. 98) How is the reversal of the Great Command an accurate portrayal of Cain's story?

   APPLY: (question 20, p. 99) What does it mean to affirm that we are "our brother's keeper"? Who should the modern-day believer view as a brother or sister? What fear, justification, or sinful attitude holds us back from treating them as such?

4. **OBSERVE:** (question 24, p. 100) Read Matthew 5:21-24. To what act does Jesus link the emotion of anger in this passage? What does Jesus say about acceptable offerings?

APPLY: (question 27, p. 101) With whom are you most likely to get angry? What would God have you do with your anger? By grace, how can you respond to it as Cain should have?

5. **WRAP-UP:** What aspect of God's character has this week's passage of Genesis shown you more clearly?

Fill in the following statement:
Knowing that God is _____ shows me that I am
_____.

What one step can you take this week to better live in light of this truth?

WEEK SIX | VIEWER GUIDE NOTES

WEEK SEVEN:

NAMED AND KNOWN

In Week Six, we watched the effects of sin on the next generation of Adam's descendants. How quickly the act of placing human will above God's will degraded into the act of murder. This week, we will watch the continued spread of wickedness along with the continuing faithfulness of God to provide redemption.

Most people don't spend much time looking at Old Testament genealogies, but we are going to take our time with them.
Start this week's lesson by looking up 2 Timothy 3:16-17.
Ask God to show you the truth of these verses as you study Genesis 4:17–6:8.

DAY ONE

READ GENESIS 4:17–6:8

1. In two or three sentences, summarize this section of the text.

2. How does this portion of the narrative connect logically to what happened in the previous chapter?

3. Which portions of this week's text were confusing to you?

DAY TWO

NOW LOOK AT GENESIS 4:17-25.

4. Look at 4:17. What project was Cain engaged in?

    _____

    Look back at the curse God placed on Cain as a result of murdering
    Abel (4:12). What does his new "building venture" suggest to you about
    the state of his heart?

5. In the table below, fill out the column with the bloodline of Cain
    found in 4:17-18.

	NAME
1	Adam
2	Cain
3	
4	
5	
6	
7	

6. In 4:19 what do we learn about Lamech, the seventh from Adam in the genealogy of Cain?

What light does this shed on his character? (See 2:24.)

7. Note Lamech's three sons and what their occupations were.

NAME	OCCUPATION

Why do you think the author includes these details in the narrative?

8. In 4:23-24 what do you learn about Lamech's character? List character traits below and your reason for noting them.

9. It is possible (but not likely) that Lamech kills in self-defense. If self-defense was his motive, which word best describes his response to being wronged?

   Justice   *Revenge*   *Mercy*

   Which of the words above *most likely* describes Lamech's true motive behind his actions? Why?

10. What is the difference between justice and revenge? Between justice and mercy? Look up these terms in a dictionary to help with your answer.

11. The number seven implied "completeness," "perfection," or "infinity" in Hebrew writing, probably because of the seven-day creation narrative. How does this idea add to your understanding of Lamech's oath in 4:24?

12. Look up Matthew 18:21-22. How does this teaching contrast with Lamech's attitude?

13. **APPLY:** Which attitude is more likely to characterize your actions when you perceive someone has wronged you?

    Justice   *Revenge*   *Mercy*

    How could you change your perception of the situation to help you demonstrate mercy instead of justice or revenge?

DAY THREE

NOW LOOK AT GENESIS 4:25-26.

14. The bloodline of Seth is introduced in this section of the text. The name *Seth* sounds like the Hebrew word for *appointed*. Based on 3:15, what do you think Eve thought Seth was appointed to do?

Was Eve correct in her assumption? Explain your answer.

15. What hopeful news do we get in 4:26? Write it below.

Look up the following verses, and note how they add to your understanding of what this phrase means:

PSALM 86:1-7

2 TIMOTHY 2:22

16. **APPLY:** Several generations pass before the righteous line of Seth begins to call upon the name of the Lord. What factors make us slow to begin to call upon Him when we are in distress or facing temptation?

In what current trial or temptation are you hesitant to call on the name of the Lord? Write it below. Commit to pray about it this week, confessing any hidden doubts or pride, and asking for grace to meet you in your time of need.

DAY FOUR

NOW LOOK AT GENESIS 5:1-32.

17. Why do you think Moses includes verse 1 of chapter 5?
    Does it sound familiar?

18. The genealogy of Seth is set in contrast to the genealogy of Cain. With whom does Moses begin the genealogy of Seth? _____
    Why do you think he does this?

19. In the spaces below, fill in the names of the genealogy of Seth.

	NAME
1	
2	
3	
4	
5	
6	
7	
8	
9	
10	

20. Note the repetition Moses uses in the genealogy of Seth. Why do you think he does not use this formula in the genealogy of Cain?

21. What repeated phrase seems most significant to you? Why do you think Moses included it?

22. Does Moses deviate from the repeated pattern at all? _____

    With which descendant? _____

    What is that person's numerical position in the line of Seth from Adam? _____

    What do you think it means that Enoch "walked faithfully with God; then he was no more, because God took him away" (v. 24, NIV)?

23. Look up Hebrews 11:5-6. How does it add to your understanding of the end of Enoch's life?

According to this passage, what did Enoch possess that allowed him to walk with God?

24. Look up the following passages and note how each adds to your understanding of "walking with God."

    PSALM 23:1-4

    1 JOHN 1:6-7

    REVELATION 3:4-5

25. In your own words, write what you think Enoch's life must have been like to be described as a walk with God. What do you think characterized his thoughts? Actions? Words?

26. **APPLY**: Walking with God implies a life of steady, worshipful obedience. What other "walking partners" are you tempted to spend time with? What would Enoch say to you about them?

DAY FIVE

NOW LOOK AT GENESIS 6:1-8.

27. Genesis 6:1-3 is notoriously difficult to interpret, and several interpretations have been put forth. We will discuss them in the teaching time. For now, do your best to draw your own conclusions by careful observation. In 6:1-2, who do you think is meant by "the sons of God"?

Who do you think is meant by "the daughters of man"?

(Hint: Think back to the curse God places on the serpent in chapter 3.)

28. What do you think is meant by 6:3? Choose the answer you think best fits the context. Explain why you chose the answer you did.

   ☐ God will shorten man's lifespan to one hundred and twenty years to punish him for his wickedness.

   ☐ God's patience with humanity's wickedness will run out in one hundred and twenty years, and He will send a flood.

29. In 6:5, note every adjective used to describe the wickedness of man. What idea does Moses want us to have about the state of things at this point in human history?

30. Look at 6:6-7. Contrast these verses to 1:31. What accounts for the dramatic change in tone between these two passages?

31. In 6:7, note, in order, the list of things that God says He will destroy.

    1. _____

    2. _____ and _____

    3. _____

    Now look back at Genesis 1, and number the order in which each of these things was created next to it. Why do you think Moses writes his narrative this way?

32. Read 6:8. Though it falls into next week's reading, go ahead and read 6:9 as well. Which of Noah's ancestors do you think he was probably most like? _____

33. Do you think that the earth is less wicked now than it was in Noah's time? Explain your answer.

34. What is your initial reaction to the text's announcement that God plans to destroy His creation? Why do you think we tend to have this reaction?

35. **APPLY:** When it comes to wickedness in our own lives, is our initial reaction to getting rid of it ever similar to the way we react to the story of the flood? Explain your answer below.

WRAP-UP

What aspect of God's character has this week's passage of Genesis shown you more clearly?

Fill in the following statement:
Knowing that God is _____ shows me that I am _____.

What one step can you take this week to better live in light of this truth?

WEEK SEVEN | GROUP DISCUSSION

INTRODUCTORY QUESTION: Who is your favorite relative, and why?

1. **OBSERVE:** (question 10, p. 113) What is the difference between justice and revenge? Between justice and mercy? Look up these terms in a dictionary to help with your answer.

   APPLY: (question 13, p. 114) Which attitude (justice, revenge, or mercy) is more likely to characterize your actions when you perceive someone has wronged you? How could you change your perception of the situation to help you demonstrate mercy instead of justice or revenge?

2. **OBSERVE:** (question 15, p. 115) What hopeful news do we get in 4:26? Look up the following verses, and note how they add to your understanding of what this phrase means: Psalm 86:1-7; 2 Timothy 2:22.

   APPLY: (question 16, p. 116) Several generations pass before the righteous line of Seth begins to call upon the name of the Lord. What factors make us slow to begin to call upon Him when we are in distress or facing temptation?

3. **OBSERVE:** (question 25, p. 120) In your own words, write what you think Enoch's life must have been like to be described as a walk with God. What do you think characterized his thoughts? Actions? Words?

   APPLY: (question 26, p. 120) Walking with God implies a life of steady, worshipful obedience. What other "walking partners" are you tempted to spend time with? What would Enoch say to you about them?

4. **OBSERVE:** (question 34, p. 122) What is your initial reaction to the text's announcement that God plans to destroy His creation? Why do you think we tend to have this reaction?

APPLY: (question 35, p. 123) When it comes to wickedness in our own lives, is our initial reaction to getting rid of it ever similar to the way we react to the story of the flood? Explain your answer.

5. **WRAP-UP:** What aspect of God's character has this week's passage of Genesis shown you more clearly?

Fill in the following statement:

Knowing that God is _____ shows me that I am

_____.

What one step can you take this week to better live in light of this truth?

WEEK SEVEN | VIEWER GUIDE NOTES

WEEK EIGHT:

THE FLOOD

In Week Seven, we saw a comparison of the unrighteous line of Cain to the righteous line of Seth. Seth's line stretches back to Adam and forward, through Noah, to Christ. This week we turn our attention to Noah, a righteous man living amidst crookedness and depravity, a man whose name significantly connotes *relief, comfort, rest*.

We will spend this week paying close attention to the structure of the narrative. Just as you did with the creation narrative of Genesis 1–2, look for patterns and repetitions as you read. Ask yourself why certain details are included while others are omitted. Ask God to give you fresh eyes and ears for a familiar story.

DAY ONE

READ GENESIS 6:9–8:19.

1. Compare 6:9 to 2:4 and 5:1. What pattern do you see?

2. Below, summarize what portion of the Genesis narrative is introduced with each of these verses.

   GENESIS 2:4

   GENESIS 5:1

   GENESIS 6:9

3. Though the story of Noah's ark may be familiar to you, what details did you notice during your reading that you had perhaps not seen before?

DAY TWO

NOW LOOK AT GENESIS 6:9-22.

4. In 6:9 we are given three phrases to describe Noah. Note each one
    below, and explain what you think it means to communicate to us
    about his character and actions.

    1. Noah was a _____ _____.

    2. Noah was _____ *in his* _____.

    3. Noah _____ *with* _____.

5. Compare 6:11-13 to 6:5-7. Why does Moses repeat himself? What is
    similar? What is different?

6. Look at 6:14-21. Note below how this passages answers the following
    questions about the ark.

    HOW:

    WHO:

WHAT:

WHERE:

WHY:

7. Now read 6:22. Why does Moses include this verse? How does it reinforce what we learned in 6:9?

8. **APPLY:** In a time of utter moral depravity, how do you think Noah stood apart from his contemporaries? How do you think his thoughts, words, and actions probably marked him distinctly as a servant of God?

Which of the markers you mentioned above do you most want to see in your own life? What keeps you from walking with God more consistently?

DAY THREE

NOW LOOK AT GENESIS 7:1-12.

9. Look at 7:2-3. Why do you think God commands Noah to bring seven pairs of clean animals and birds instead of just two? (Hint: Peek ahead at next week's text.)

10. What idea does 7:5 reinforce?

11. How old was Noah when he entered the ark? _____

    Look back at 5:32. How old was Noah when his sons were born?

    _____

    Based on this information, estimate how long you think it probably took Noah to build the ark: _____

    Look at 7:7,13. How many humans were spared inside the ark?

    _____

12. Based on 7:8-9, how is God's command to Noah to fill the ark with animals accomplished?

13. **APPLY:** What lessons can you draw from your answers to question 11? How does the God-ordained chronology of Noah's story shape or change your perspective on your own life?

NOW LOOK AT GENESIS 7:13-24.

14. Look carefully through this passage for any ideas, phrases, or images that sound familiar. Note them below. Look back to Genesis 1–2, and note where you first heard them.

FAMILIAR IDEAS, PHRASES, OR IMAGES	GENESIS 1–2 CROSS-REFERENCE

Why do you think Moses reuses these ideas in the flood story?

15. How would you describe the tone of 7:11-16? Summarize its main idea into one sentence.

16. How would you describe the tone of 7:17-24? Summarize its main idea into one sentence.

17. Look up Hebrews 11:7. In the space below, note how Noah is described:

By _____ Noah, being warned by God concerning events as yet

unseen, in _____ _____ constructed an ark for

the saving of his household. By this he _____ _____

_____ and became an heir of the righteousness that comes

by faith.

What evidence from Noah's story in Genesis supports this description of him?

18. **APPLY:** What do you think it means to be characterized by "reverent fear" as we go about the work of the Lord? How well does that phrase describe your own disposition as a believer?

NOW LOOK AT GENESIS 8:1-14.

19. In Genesis 7–8 we are given a chronology of the flood. In the chart below, outline that chronology:

VERSE	TIME PERIOD	WHAT HAPPENED
Genesis 7:4,10		
Genesis 7:12,17		
Genesis 7:24; 8:3		
Genesis 8:5-6		
Genesis 8:10		
Genesis 8:12		

Look again at your chart. Count how many different time periods, or stages, of the flood are mentioned: _____

Do you see any significance in that number? (Think back to the creation story in Genesis 1.)

20. Read Psalm 69:1-16. Who wrote this psalm? _____.
Who could just as easily have written this psalm? Why? Note any phrases or thoughts that support your answer below.

21. **APPLY:** Now think about your own life. Have you ever been through a "flood"? Describe that time below. In what way does your story mirror Noah's? How is it different? What did you learn about God, yourself, and others as a result?

WRAP-UP

What aspect of God's character has this week's passage of Genesis shown you more clearly?

Fill in the following statement:

Knowing that God is _____ shows me that I am

_____.

What one step can you take this week to better live in light of this truth?

INTRODUCTORY QUESTION: Describe a time when you were impacted by a natural disaster or act of nature.

1. **OBSERVE:** (question 7, p. 132) Read 6:22. Why does Moses include this verse? How does it reinforce what we learned in 6:9?

   APPLY: (question 8, p. 132) In a time of utter moral depravity, how do you think Noah stood apart from his contemporaries? How do you think his thoughts, words, and actions probably marked him distinctly as a servant of God?

   Which of the markers you mentioned do you most want to see in your own life? What keeps you from walking with God more consistently?

2. **OBSERVE:** (question 11, p. 133) How old was Noah when he entered the ark? Look back at 5:32. How old was Noah when his sons were born?

   Based on this information, estimate how long you think it probably took Noah to build the ark.

   Look at 7:7,13. How many humans were spared inside the ark?

   APPLY: (question 13, p. 133) What lessons can you draw from your answers to question 11 (p. 133)? How does the God-ordained chronology of Noah's story shape or change your perspective on your own life?

3. **OBSERVE:** (question 17, p. 135) Look up Hebrews 11:7. Note how Noah is described. What evidence from Noah's story in Genesis supports this description of him?

APPLY: (question 18, p. 135) What do you think it means to be characterized by "reverent fear" as we go about the work of the Lord? How well does that phrase describe your own disposition as a believer?

4. **OBSERVE:** (question 20, p. 136) Read Psalm 69:1-16. Who wrote this psalm? Who could just as easily have written this psalm? Why? Note any phrases or thoughts that support your answer.

APPLY: (question 21, p. 137) Now think about your own life. Have you ever been through a "flood"? Describe that time. In what way does your story mirror Noah's? How is it different? What did you learn about God, yourself, and others as a result?

5. **WRAP-UP:** What aspect of God's character has this week's passage of Genesis shown you more clearly?

Fill in the following statement:
Knowing that God is _____ shows me that I am
_____.

What one step can you take this week to better live in light of this truth?

WEEK EIGHT | VIEWER GUIDE NOTES

WEEK NINE:

GOD'S COVENANT WITH NOAH

In Week Eight, we followed Noah and his family through the floodwaters. When we wrapped up our time together last week, the passengers of the ark were about to emerge into the sunlight of a post-flood Earth. Imagine having spent over a year enclosed in a boat, tasked with the care of a large zoo, unsure of how long you must wait or what would await you once the flood waters subsided. At last the ground is dry, and you emerge from the darkness of the ark into daylight. What do you think Noah and his family saw as their eyes adjusted to the scene around them?

READ THROUGH GENESIS 8:15–9:29. THEN LOOK BACK AT
8:13-19. TRY TO SEE THE SCENE THROUGH NOAH'S EYES.

1. Think about the most recent natural disaster you can remember
   seeing in person or on the news. How did those images and stories
   make you feel? Below, note specifically how you felt about …

THE PHYSICAL DESTRUCTION OF PROPERTY AND NATURE

THE LOSS OF HUMAN LIFE

2. Now compare that natural disaster to the flood that Noah survived.
   How are they the same? How are they different?

	NOAH'S FLOOD	RECENT NATURAL DISASTER
Similarities		
Differences		

How do you think Noah felt about the scene waiting for him at the bottom of the gangplank?

3. Look again at 8:15-19. Look carefully at the first phrase of 8:15 and 8:18. How does it remind you of Genesis 1?

4. Read Psalm 29. Note each thing the psalm says the voice of the Lord is or *does*. Write the ideas that stand out to you the most below.

5. Now look up the following verses, and note how each reinforces the message of Psalm 29.
    1 SAMUEL 2:6-7

    ECCLESIASTES 7:13

ISAIAH 45:5-7

LAMENTATIONS 3:37-38

6. Look back at Psalm 29. What do you think verses 10-11 communicate about God's role in times of disaster?

7. **APPLY:** What seems to be the psalmist's response to God's role in times of disaster (29:1-2)?

How do you think Noah felt toward God in his time of disaster?

What is your response to God's role in times of disaster? What do you think is the right response?

DAY TWO

NOW LOOK AT GENESIS 8:20-22.

8. According to verse 20, what is the first thing that Noah does upon exiting the ark?

If you had just spent over a year confined to a boat, enduring seasickness and smelly animals, only to step off the boat into a post-flood wasteland, what would your first act have been? List some possibilities below.

What does Noah's sacrifice indicate about his heart?

9. In 8:21-22, God responds to the Noah's sacrifice with several statements. Look back at 6:18. What is the name for the type of promise that God makes to Noah? _____

Look up this term in a dictionary or thesaurus, and write a definition for it below that best fits the context of the passage.

COVENANT:

10. The concept of covenant is central to our understanding of God and of our salvation. We have already seen an implied covenant between God and Adam in Genesis 2:15-17. Look back at those verses and answer the questions below.

	ADAMIC COVENANT
Who initiates the covenant?	
Which two parties are involved in the covenant?	
What does God promise? (Think about Eden.)	
What is required of Adam?	
What is the penalty for breach of the covenant?	

11. **APPLY:** What is the best faithfully-kept promise you have ever received from another person? In the space below, note who promised, what was promised, what was required of you, and how the promise has been fulfilled.

How is the promise-keeping of God better than even the best human promise? Note at least three ways below.

DAY THREE

Before we look more closely at the covenant with Noah, let's dig into the text. You will need colored pens or pencils for this section of the homework.

READ THROUGH 8:20–9:19 IN THE COPY OF THIS WEEK'S TEXT PRINTED AT THE END OF THE WEEK NINE HOMEWORK (P. 155).

12. With a **green** pen, highlight every reference to *the LORD, God,* and every time God speaks of Himself with the pronouns *I, me, my,* or *mine.*

    What does the presence of all those **green** marks tell you about Moses' portrayal of God's role in this section of the Genesis narrative?

    Do the words in **green** tend to indicate the *subject* or the *object* of the narrative?

13. Now mark in **red** every occurrence of the term *never.*

    Which character in the narrative uses this word repeatedly?

    _____

    Why is that significant to our understanding of the text?

14. Mark in **blue** every occurrence of the words *all, every,* or *everything.* Mark in **orange** every occurrence of *man* or *you.* Do the words in **blue** and **orange** tend to indicate the *subject* or the *object* of the narrative?

15. Now, look at the covenant God makes with Noah in 8:21-22; 9:8-9. Answer the following questions.

	NOAHIC COVENANT
Who initiates the covenant? (green words)	
Which parties are involved in the covenant? (green, blue, orange words)	
What does God promise? (red words)	
What is required of Noah?	
What is the penalty for breach of the covenant?	

16. What is the sign of the covenant God makes with Noah (9:12)?

What two weather conditions are necessary for this sign to occur? Circle them below.

Rain   *Snow*   *Hail*   *Sunlight*   *Tornado*

Look up John 8:12. How does Jesus describe Himself?

How does this image expand your understanding of the sign of His faithfulness that God gives to Noah?

17. What provoked God to flood the earth in the first place? _____

According to 8:21, will the post-flood world be different than the pre-flood world? Why or why not?

Why do you think God flooded the earth if sin still lived in the hearts of Noah and his descendants?

18. Compare 9:1-3 to Genesis 1:28-30. How are these passages similar? Different?

19. The shedding of blood is an idea central to our understanding of the gospel. In 9:4-6 note what God says about blood and bloodshed. How do His words build on the idea of atonement?

20. Think back on God's response toward Cain, the murderer. What was Cain's punishment?

According to 9:6, what will be the punishment for murder in the post-flood world?

Why do you think this punishment is put in place?

21. **APPLY:** The story of the flood is commonly understood to be a picture of God's wrath and justice. How might we see it also as a picture of His mercy and grace?

DAY FOUR

NOW LOOK AT 9:18-29.

22. In this colorful story, how do we find Noah behaving?

23. When was the last time we encountered nakedness in Genesis?

    What emotion was associated with nakedness at that time?

    What was God's solution to the nakedness of Adam and Eve?

24. Compare Ham's reaction to his father's nakedness to the reaction of his brothers. In the space below, explain what you think is going on in this weird little story.

25. Look at Noah's reaction to his treatment. Note what he says about each of his sons' family lines.
    HAM (CANAAN'S FATHER):

    SHEM:

    JAPHETH:

26. Based on what you know of the history of the nation of Israel, does Noah's curse stick? (We'll go over this in the teaching time, so don't panic if you're a little fuzzy on this.)

27. **APPLY:** What can we learn from Noah's almost immediate lapse into sin after being brought safely through the waters of God's judgment on sinners? How should his story warn us?

How should Hebrews 11:7 reassure us?

WRAP-UP

What aspect of God's character has this week's passage of Genesis shown you more clearly?

Fill in the following statement:
Knowing that God is _____ shows me that I am
_____.

What one step can you take this week to better live in light of this truth?

GENESIS 8:15-22

[15] Then God said to Noah, [16] "Go out from the ark, you and your wife, and your sons and your sons' wives with you. [17] Bring out with you every living thing that is with you of all flesh—birds and animals and every creeping thing that creeps on the earth—that they may swarm on the earth, and be fruitful and multiply on the earth." [18] So Noah went out, and his sons and his wife and his sons' wives with him. [19] Every beast, every creeping thing, and every bird, everything that moves on the earth, went out by families from the ark.

[20] Then Noah built an altar to the LORD and took some of every clean animal and some of every clean bird and offered burnt offerings on the altar. [21] And when the LORD smelled the pleasing aroma, the LORD said in his heart, "I will never again curse the ground because of man, for the intention of man's heart is evil from his youth. Neither will I ever again strike down every living creature as I have done. [22] While the earth remains, seedtime and harvest, cold and heat, summer and winter, day and night, shall not cease."

GENESIS 9

[1] And God blessed Noah and his sons and said to them, "Be fruitful and multiply and fill the earth. [2] The fear of you and the dread of you shall be upon every beast of the earth and upon every bird of the heavens, upon everything that creeps on the ground and all the fish of the sea. Into your hand they are delivered. [3] Every moving thing that lives shall be food for you. And as I gave you the green plants, I give you everything. [4] But you shall not eat flesh with its life, that is, its blood. [5] And for your lifeblood I will require a reckoning: from every beast I will require it and from man. From his fellow man I will require a reckoning for the life of man.

6 "Whoever sheds the blood of man,

    by man shall his blood be shed,

  for God made man in his own image.

7 And you, be fruitful and multiply, teem on the earth and multiply in it."

8 Then God said to Noah and to his sons with him, 9 "Behold, I establish my covenant with you and your offspring after you, 10 and with every living creature that is with you, the birds, the livestock, and every beast of the earth with you, as many as came out of the ark; it is for every beast of the earth. 11 I establish my covenant with you, that never again shall all flesh be cut off by the waters of the flood, and never again shall there be a flood to destroy the earth." 12 And God said, "This is the sign of the covenant that I make between me and you and every living creature that is with you, for all future generations: 13 I have set my bow in the cloud, and it shall be a sign of the covenant between me and the earth. 14 When I bring clouds over the earth and the bow is seen in the clouds, 15 I will remember my covenant that is between me and you and every living creature of all flesh. And the waters shall never again become a flood to destroy all flesh. 16 When the bow is in the clouds, I will see it and remember the everlasting covenant between God and every living creature of all flesh that is on the earth." 17 God said to Noah, "This is the sign of the covenant that I have established between me and all flesh that is on the earth."

18 The sons of Noah who went forth from the ark were Shem, Ham, and Japheth. (Ham was the father of Canaan.) 19 These three were the sons of Noah, and from these the people of the whole earth were dispersed.

20 Noah began to be a man of the soil, and he planted a vineyard. 21 He drank of the wine and became drunk and lay uncovered in his tent. 22 And Ham, the father of Canaan, saw the nakedness of his father and told his

two brothers outside. ²³ Then Shem and Japheth took a garment, laid it on both their shoulders, and walked backward and covered the nakedness of their father. Their faces were turned backward, and they did not see their father's nakedness. ²⁴ When Noah awoke from his wine and knew what his youngest son had done to him, ²⁵ he said,

"Cursed be Canaan;
    a servant of servants shall he be to his brothers."

²⁶ He also said,
  "Blessed be the LORD, the God of Shem;
      and let Canaan be his servant.
  ²⁷ May God enlarge Japheth,
      and let him dwell in the tents of Shem,
      and let Canaan be his servant."

²⁸ After the flood Noah lived 350 years. ²⁹ All the days of Noah were 950 years, and he died.

INTRODUCTORY QUESTION: What is the longest trip you've ever taken?

1. OBSERVE: (question 4 & 6, pp. 145-146) Read Psalm 29. Note each thing the psalm says the voice of the Lord is or *does*. Which ideas stand out to you the most? What do you think verses 10-11 communicate about God's role in times of disaster?

APPLY: (question 7, p. 146) What seems to be the psalmist's response to God's role in times of disaster (29:1-2)?

How do you think Noah felt toward God in his time of disaster?

What is your response to God's role in times of disaster? What do you think is the right response?

2. OBSERVE: (question 9, p. 147) Share and compare the definitions you wrote for the word *covenant*. Discuss why you chose the definition you did.

APPLY: (question 11, p. 148) What is the best faithfully-kept promise you have ever received from another person?

How is the promise-keeping of God better than even the best human promise?

3. OBSERVE: (question 17, p. 151) What provoked God to flood the earth in the first place?

According to 8:21, will the post-flood world be different than the pre-flood world? Why or why not?

Why do you think God flooded the earth if sin still lived in the hearts of Noah and his descendants?

APPLY: (question 21, p. 152) The story of the flood is commonly understood to be a picture of God's wrath and justice. How might we see it also as a picture of His mercy and grace?

4. **OBSERVE:** (question 24, p. 153) Compare Ham's reaction to his father's nakedness to the reaction of his brothers. Discuss your explanations of what you think is going on in this weird little story.

APPLY: (question 27, p. 154) What can we learn from Noah's almost immediate lapse into sin after being brought safely through the waters of God's judgment on sinners? How should his story warn us?

How should Hebrews 11:7 reassure us?

5. **WRAP-UP:** What aspect of God's character has this week's passage of Genesis shown you more clearly?

Fill in the following statement:
Knowing that God is _____ shows me that I am
_____.

What one step can you take this week to better live in light of this truth?

WEEK NINE | VIEWER GUIDE NOTES

WEEK TEN:

DISPERSION AND DESCENT

In Week Nine, we watched Noah, the preacher of righteousness, become the participant in a God-initiated, God-sustained covenant. We also watched as this second Adam descended into sin, resulting in a curse on his son's son. This week we will examine the curse on Ham's son Canaan and his descendants. We'll also see how long the memory of widespread devastation kept Earth's inhabitants from sin. And we'll trace the path of Noah's descendants all the way to Abram, the father of the nation of Israel.

DAY ONE

READ GENESIS 10:1–11:32.

1. Write a one-sentence summary of each section of this week's text.
   GENESIS 10

   GENESIS 11:1-9

   GENESIS 11:10-26

   GENESIS 11:27-32

2. How does this week's section serve as a bridge between the flood narrative and the story of Abram, which begins in chapter 12?

DAY TWO

NOW LOOK AT GENESIS 10. YOU MAY BE TEMPTED TO
SKIM, BUT READ CAREFULLY. GENEALOGIES MATTER!

3. Note the familiar phrasing of 10:1, indicating we are entering a new
    section of the story of Genesis. According to this verse, which three
    family lines will be traced in this chapter?

4. Glancing through the listings, what general kinds of information do
    you learn about each family line? Summarize.

5. In order to understand the connections between Noah's family
    members and his prophetic words in Genesis 9:18-29, let's piece
    together some relationships. Note the names of Noah's sons
    below (10:1).

    1. _____

    2. _____

    3. _____

    Look back at Genesis 9:18-29. Upon whom did Noah prophetically
    proclaim a curse (9:24-25)?

    _____, who is the son of _____ and the
    grandson of _____

    Now, compare Genesis 10:6. Ham's sons are listed in birth order. Which
    son is the youngest? _____

Ham, the youngest of his brothers, becomes a source of shame to his father. In terms of family relationships, how is Noah's curse fitting to Ham's offense?

6. According to 10:6, how many sons did Ham have in all? _____

In light of this information, how was Noah's curse less harsh than it could have been?

In his curse, Noah repeats three times what the fate of Canaan's descendants will be. What is that fate?

7. Below is a map of the territories of the descendants of Noah's sons. Search through the genealogies for each name. On the map, highlight the descendants of Shem in **yellow**, Ham in **orange**, and Japheth in **blue**.

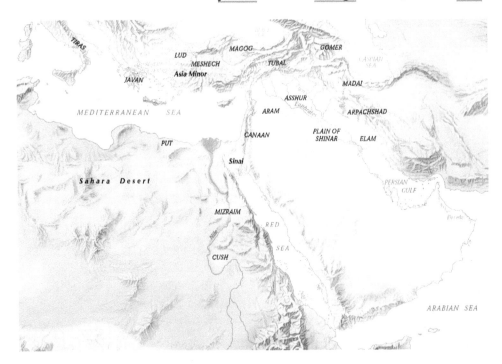

Does the map look familiar? Note that Tiras is on the boot of modern-day Italy, extending into the Mediterranean Ocean. Mizraim is the Hebrew name for Egypt.

8. Look at the region in which each son's descendants are grouped. Match the name of the son to his region below:

Shem   Indo-European

Ham   Middle-eastern/Persian

Japheth   African/Canaanite

9. Look back at Genesis 9:26. Which of Noah's sons is singled out to have the Lord as his God? _____

    Have you ever heard the term anti-semitic? It is used to refer to hatred toward the Jews. This is because another name for the Jewish people is the Semites. What do you think is the origin of this name?

    How does this add to your understanding of the significance of Noah's blessing in 9:26?

10. Remember that Moses is writing Genesis to the Israelites to prepare them for life in the promised land, the land of Canaan. They will be commanded to go into Canaan and subdue it completely. The Canaanites were a particularly perverse and sinful people group. Just how bad were they? Take a look at Leviticus 18:1-28. List below some of the detestable practices that characterized the Canaanites.

11. Now look up the following passages, and note how God commanded the Israelites to deal with the Canaanites.

DEUTERONOMY 7:1-6

DEUTERONOMY 12:1-3

DEUTERONOMY 18:9-12

12. What was the danger to the Israelites that these people and their practices posed?

13. **APPLY:** How are we in similar danger today? What are some modern-day ways in which close proximity to sin threatens our faithfulness to God? List specific examples, and note how we might effectively conquer them as the people of God.

NOW READ GENESIS 11:1-9.

14. Based on 11:1, what implied question does the story of Babel seek to answer?

15. Does this story seem to be in chronological sequence in the narrative? Why or why not? Cite specific verses from chapter 10 to support your answer. (Hint: There are three.)

16. Re-read 11:3-4. Specifically, what did the men in this story want to do?

    11:3 *"Come, let us _____."*

    11:4 *"Come, let us _____."*

    "... and let us _____."

17. Do you see any significance to the pattern of speech Moses gives the men? Compare the language of Genesis 1:26 to 11:3-4.

	WHO IS SPEAKING?	WHAT IS BEING CREATED?
Genesis 1:26		
Genesis 11:3-4		

What does Moses want to show us about the motives of these men by their speech pattern?

18. **APPLY:** In 11:4, the men give three goals for wanting to build the city and tower. They are listed below. Next to each one, write what sinful attitudes, fears, or values might generate such a goal.

TO REACH THE HEAVENS

TO MAKE A NAME FOR THEMSELVES

TO AVOID BEING SCATTERED OVER THE FACE OF THE EARTH

How do we chase after similar goals today?

19. What kind of tower did the men want to build (11:4)?

    ESV: *"a tower with* _____ *... "*

    NIV: *"a tower that* _____ *... "*

    How does 11:5 indicate that they did not achieve their goal?

20. What significant language repetition occurs in 11:7? Based on who is speaking, why is it used?

21. According to 11:6, why did God thwart the people's attempt at united accomplishment?

22. Look up the following verses, and note what they say about building and unity.

    EPHESIANS 2:11-22

    EPHESIANS 4:1-16

How is God's concept of beneficial unity different from man's?

23. **APPLY:** Now reflect on your own life. In what ways are you a tower-builder, striving to build something that will show your abilities or establish your significance?

In what ways are you a city-builder, striving to accumulate or control?

DAY FIVE

NOW LOOK AT GENESIS 11:10-32.

25. How does this set of genealogies compare to the one we saw in
    Genesis 5? What is similar? What is different?

26. Compare the opening statements of each of the following verses:

	THESE ARE THE GENERATIONS OF ...
Genesis 2:4	... the _____ and the _____ ...
Genesis 6:9	... _____.
Genesis 10:1	... the _____ of _____, _____, _____, and _____.
Genesis 11:10	... _____.
Genesis 11:27	... _____. _____ fathered _____.

How does Moses use this repeated formula to bring an increasingly
narrow focus to his narrative?

26. **APPLY:** Genesis 12–50 will outline the lives of Abram (Abraham) and his descendants, the fledgling nation of Israel. In Genesis 1–11, Moses has skillfully walked us from the birth of the world to the birth of a nation, indicating God's sovereign hand throughout. God orders both the big story of salvation and the small stories of our individual lives. How have you seen God's sovereign hand ordering your own life and story?

WRAP-UP

What aspect of God's character has this week's passage of Genesis shown you more clearly?

Fill in the following statement:
Knowing that God is _____ shows me that I am
_____.

What one step can you take this week to better live in light of this truth?

WEEK TEN | GROUP DISCUSSION

INTRODUCTORY QUESTION: Do you speak any language(s) other than English? If so, how well and why?

1. **OBSERVE:** (questions 12 & 13, p. 169) Note how God commanded the Israelites to deal with the Canaanites in Deuteronomy 7:1-6; 12:1-3; 18:9-12.

   What was the danger to the Israelites that these people and their practices posed?

   APPLY: (question 14, p. 169) How are we in similar danger today? What are some modern-day ways in which close proximity to sin threatens our faithfulness to God? List specific examples, and note how we might effectively conquer them as the people of God.

2. **OBSERVE:** (question 16, p. 170) Does the story of Babel seem to be in chronological sequence in the narrative? Why or why not? Cite specific verses from chapter 10 to support your answer. (Hint: There are three.)

   APPLY: (question 19, p. 171) In 11:4, the men give three goals for wanting to build the city and tower: to reach the heavens, to make a name for themselves, to avoid being scattered over the face of the earth. What sinful attitudes, fears, or values might generate such goals? How do we chase after similar goals today?

3. **OBSERVE:** (questions 22 & 23, p. 172) According to 11:6, why did God thwart the people's attempt at united accomplishment?

   Based on Ephesians 2:11-22 and 4:1-16, how is God's concept of beneficial unity different from man's?

APPLY: (question 24, p. 173) Now reflect on your own life. In what ways are you a tower-builder, striving to build something that will show your abilities or establish your significance? In what ways are you a city-builder, striving to accumulate or control?

4. **OBSERVE:** (question 26, p. 174) How does Moses use the repeated formula of "These are the generations of ... " to bring an increasingly narrow focus to his narrative?

APPLY: (question 27, p. 175) Genesis 12–50 will outline the lives of Abram (Abraham) and his descendants, the fledgling nation of Israel. In Genesis 1–11, Moses has skillfully walked us from the birth of the world to the birth of a nation, indicating God's sovereign hand throughout. God orders both the big story of salvation and the small stories of our individual lives. How have you seen God's sovereign hand ordering your own life and story?

5. **WRAP-UP:** What aspect of God's character has this week's passage of Genesis shown you more clearly?

Fill in the following statement:
Knowing that God is _____ shows me that I am

_____ .

What one step can you take this week to better live in light of this truth?

WEEK TEN | VIEWER GUIDE NOTES

WRAP-UP

You've made it! You have walked faithfully through the eleven chapters of the primeval history of the world. Having spent the last ten weeks digging in the fertile soil that is the "seed plot of the Bible," it's time now to reflect on what seeds we have seen planted there.

Here is an optional wrap-up session to help you process what you've learned and keep the big picture in mind.

READ STRAIGHT THROUGH GENESIS 1–11.

As you read, think back on what you have learned in these newly-familiar pages. Answer the following questions.

1. What attribute of God has emerged most clearly as you have studied these chapters?

    How does knowing this truth about Him change the way you see yourself?

    How should knowing this truth change the way you live?

2. How has the Holy Spirit used Genesis 1–11 to convict you of sin? What thoughts, words, or actions has He shown you that need to be redeemed? What do you need to stop doing?

3. How has the Holy Spirit used Genesis 1–11 to train you in righteousness? What disciplines has He given you a desire to pursue? What do you need to start doing?

4. How has the Holy Spirit used Genesis 1–11 to encourage you? What cause to celebrate have these chapters imprinted on your heart?

5. Which familiar story of Genesis 1–11 took on deeper meaning for you? In what way?

6. Which previously unfamiliar story or passage stands out in your mind the most? Why?

7. Where did you see Christ most clearly in the Genesis narrative (John 5:46-47)?

Close in prayer. Thank God that from the earliest pages of His Word redemption was clearly in His view. Ask Him to give you eyes to see how the words of Genesis inform and enrich the words of the rest of Scripture. Confess your great need of Him, of salvation. Thank Him that provision has been made for your need—not in Adam, nor Seth, nor Enoch, nor Noah, nor in any righteous man, but in the flawless righteousness of the Last Adam, the God-Man Jesus. The serpent's head is crushed indeed—thanks be to God!

THE ATTRIBUTES OF GOD

Attentive: God hears and responds to the needs of His children.

Compassionate: God cares for His children and acts on their behalves.

Creator: God made everything. He is uncreated.

Deliverer: God rescues and saves His children.

Eternal: God is not limited by and exists outside of time.

Faithful: God always keeps His promises.

Generous: God gives what is best and beyond what is deserved.

Glorious: God displays His greatness and worth.

Good: God is what is best and gives what is best. He is incapable of doing harm.

Holy: God is perfect, pure, and without sin.

Incomprehensible: God is beyond our understanding. We can comprehend Him in part but not in whole.

Infinite: God has no limits in His person or on His power.

Immutable/Unchanging: God never changes. He is the same yesterday, today, and tomorrow.

Jealous: God will not share His glory with another. All glory rightfully belongs to Him.

Just: God is fair in all His actions and judgments. He cannot over-punish or under-punish.

Loving: God feels and displays infinite, unconditional affection toward His children. His love for them does not depend on their worth, response, or merit.

Merciful: God does not give His children the punishment they deserve.

Omnipotent/Almighty: God holds all power. Nothing is too hard for God. What He wills He can accomplish.

Omnipresent: God is fully present everywhere.

Omniscient: God knows everything, past, present, and future, all potential and real outcomes, all things micro and macro.

Patient/Long-suffering: God is untiring and bears with His children

Provider: God meets the needs of His children.

Refuge: God is a place of safety and protection for His children.

Righteous: God is always good and right.

Self-existent: God depends on nothing and no one to give Him life or existence.

Self-sufficient: God is not vulnerable. He has no needs.

Sovereign: God does everything according to His plan and pleasure. He controls all things.

Transcendent: God is not like humans. He is infinitely higher in being and action.

Truthful: Whatever God speaks or does is truth and reality.

Wrathful: God hates all unrighteousness.

Wise: God knows what is best and acts accordingly. He cannot choose wrongly.

Worthy: God deserves all glory and honor and praise.

SOURCES CONSULTED IN THE CREATION OF THIS STUDY

Arthur W. Pink, *Gleanings In Genesis, Volume 1* (Chicago: Moody Bible Institute of Chicago, 1922).

Bill T. Arnold, *Encountering the Book of Genesis* (Grand Rapids, MI: Baker Academic, 1998).

J. Ligon Duncan, III; David W. Hall; Hugh Ross; Gleason L. Archer; Lee Irons; Meredith G. Kline, *The Genesis Debate: Three Views on the Days of Creation* (Mission Viejo, CA: Crux Press, Inc., 2001).

James Montgomery Boice, *Genesis, An Expositional Commentary, Volume 1: Genesis 1–11* (Grand Rapids, MI: Baker Books, 1982).

Justin Taylor "How Old Is the Universe?" *The Gospel Coalition Blog* February 5, 2014 *https://www.thegospelcoalition.org/blogs/justin-taylor/how-old-is-the-universe/*.

Paul Nelson, Robert C. Newman, Howard J. Van Till, *Three Views on Creation and Evolution* (Grand Rapids, MI: Zondervan, 1999).

Paul Wright, Ed. *Shepherd's Notes: Genesis* (Nashville: B&H Publishing Group, 1997).

The Navigators, *Genesis, Volume 16 of the LifeChange Series* (Colorado Springs, Colorado: NavPress Publishing Group, 1987).

Tim Keller, "Sinned in a Literal Adam, Raised in a Literal Christ" *The Gospel Coalition Blog* June 6, 2011 *https://www.thegospelcoalition.org/article/sinned-in-a-literal-adam-raised-in-a-literal-christ/*.

ENDNOTES

WEEK TWO

1. J. Ligon Duncan, III; David W. Hall; Hugh Ross; Gleason L. Archer; Lee Irons; Meredith G. Kline, *The Genesis Debate: Three Views on the Days of Creation* (Mission Viejo, CA: Crux Press, Inc., 2001), 101.

2. Ibid.

3. Karisa Schlehr, "What Is R.C. Sproul's Position on Creation?" *Ligoner Ministries* February 9, 2011 *http://www.ligonier.org/blog/what-rc-sprouls-position-creation/.*

4. Kenneth D. Keathley and Mark F. Rooker, *40 Questions About Creation and Evolution* (Grand Rapids, MI: Kregel Publications, 2014), 15.

   "How is BioLogos different from Evolutionism, Intelligent Design, and Creationism?" *Biologos http://biologos.org/common-questions/christianity-and-science/biologos-id-creationism/.*

5. Paul Nelson, Robert C. Newman, Howard J. Van Till, *Three Views on Creation and Evolution* (Grand Rapids, MI: Zondervan, 1999).

6. Wayne Grudem, *Systematic Theology* (Grand Rapids, MI: Zondervan and Leicester, Great Britain: Inter-Varsity Press, England, 1994), 295.

   Denis O. Lamoureux, *Evolutionary Creation: A Christian Approach to Evolution* (England: The Lutterworth Press, 2008), 22.

7. Lamoureux, 26-27.

8. Grudem, 298.

9. Grudem, 300.

NOTES

LET'S BE FRIENDS!

BLOG

We're here to help you grow in your faith, develop as a leader, and find encouragement as you go.

lifewaywomen.com

SOCIAL

Find inspiration in the in-between moments of life.

@lifewaywomen

NEWSLETTER

Be the first to hear about new studies, events, giveaways, and more by signing up.

lifeway.com/womensnews

APP

Download the Lifeway Women app for Bible study plans, online study groups, a prayer wall, and more!

 Google Play   App Store

Lifeway women

OTHER STUDIES BY JEN WILKIN

BETTER
10 Sessions

Explore the Book of Hebrews to learn how to place your hope and faith in Christ alone.

lifeway.com/better

1 PETER
9 Sessions

Study the Book of 1 Peter to look beyond your current circumstances to a future inheritance through Christ.

lifeway.com/1peterstudy

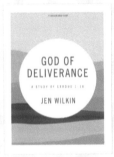

GOD OF DELIVERANCE
10 Sessions

Discover the same God who delivered Israel will also deliver you from slavery to sin and from service to the pharaohs of this world.

lifeway.com/deliverance

GOD OF COVENANT
10 Sessions

Walk alongside the fathers of our faith in Genesis 12–50—Abraham, Isaac, Jacob, and Joseph—to discern Jesus in the stories of His people.

lifeway.com/godofcovenant

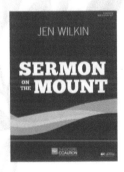

SERMON ON THE MOUNT
9 Sessions

Study Jesus' Sermon on the Mount verse by verse to learn what it means to be a citizen of the kingdom of heaven.

lifeway.com/sermononthemount

lifeway.com/jenwilkin | 800.458.2772

Lifeway women

Pricing and availability subject to change without notice.

Get the most from your study.

Customize your Bible study time with a guided experience.

Over 10 sessions of verse-by-verse study, dive into the first 11 chapters of Genesis by following three critical stages of understanding: comprehension, interpretation, and application. Revisit familiar stories and historical figures, challenge your basic knowledge, and discover deeper meanings in the text. As God reveals Himself through Scripture, we can only begin to understand ourselves when we first glimpse the character, attributes, and promises of our Creator.

In this study you'll:

- Discover what the Bible says about God, His character, and attributes.

- Learn to love God with your mind as well as your heart through intentional study.

- Challenge your basic understanding of familiar stories through three critical stages of understanding: comprehension, interpretation, and application.

- Gain knowledge of yourself by first understanding God as He has revealed Himself through Scripture.

Jen's teaching sessions are essential for the learning impact of the study. This study book is written to prepare you for the teachings, not to stand alone. Each 30–35-minute session unpacks fundamental truths taught in *God of Creation* and clarifies your study time questions.

Studying on your own or with a friend? Watch or listen to Jen's teaching sessions as you study, available for rent or purchase at lifeway.com/creation.

Leading a group? Our leader kits are designed for leaders and make it easy to get your group started (leader kit includes one *God of Creation* Bible study book, DVDs with teaching videos, and teaching video downloads for 3 additional users). Get yours at lifeway.com/creation.

ADDITIONAL RESOURCES

Visit lifeway.com/creation to explore the entire study family—Bible study book, leader kit, Bible study eBook, video teaching sessions, and audio teaching sessions—along with a free session sample, video clips, and church promotional materials.